PRAISE FOR

Laughter in the Dark

"*Laughter in the Dark* is a brilliantly composed portrait of Egypt's answer to hip-hop—and how it functions as a musical genre, economic engine, and cultural force amid the restrictions of an increasingly authoritarian regime. Meticulously reported and elegantly written, it's a must-read for any global citizen."
—ZACK O'MALLEY GREENBURG,
author of *Empire State of Mind:
How Jay-Z Went From Street Corner to Corner Office*

"The year 2011 brought revolutionary dreams to the forefront of Egyptian politics, but subsequent years have been cruel to those dreams. If we move from day-to-day politics to generational change, we see something very different: a repressive regime face-to-face with irrepressible cultural efflorescence. Yasmine El Rashidi guides us to look far from the headlines and consider the creative energies that make Egypt more than a site of dashed hopes."
—NATHAN J. BROWN,
professor of political science and international affairs,
George Washington University

"In *Laughter in the Dark*, Yasmine El Rashidi provides a brisk, brilliant, and brave portrait of young Egyptians simmering under the weight of President Abdel Fattah El-Sisi's repressive dictatorship and reveals the stark inequality between the rulers and the ruled."
—BASHARAT PEER,
author of *A Question of Order:
India, Turkey, and the Return of Strongmen*

Laughter in
the Dark
Egypt to the
Tune of Change

COLUMBIA GLOBAL REPORTS
NEW YORK

Laughter in
the Dark
Egypt to the
Tune of Change

Yasmine El Rashidi

0 Miles 20 40
0 Kilometers 40 80

Mediterranean Sea

Alexandria

North Coast

© 2023 Jeffrey L. Ward

Egypt

★ Cairo

● New Administrative Capital

Nile R.

Nile R.

In memory of Bob Silvers

Published with support from the Andrew W. Mellon Foundation

Laughter in the Dark
Egypt to the Tune of Change
Copyright © 2023 by Yasmine El Rashidi
All rights reserved

Published by Columbia Global Reports
91 Claremont Avenue, Suite 515
New York, NY 10027
globalreports.columbia.edu
facebook.com/columbiaglobalreports
@columbiaGR

Library of Congress Cataloging-in-Publication Data

Names: El Rashidi, Yasmine, 1977- author.
Title: Laughter in the dark : Egypt to the tune of change / Yasmine El Rashidi.
Description: New York : Columbia Global Reports, 2023. | Includes
    bibliographical references.
Identifiers: LCCN 2023011759 (print) | LCCN 2023011760 (ebook) |
    ISBN 9798987053508 (paperback) | ISBN 9798987053515 (ebook)
Subjects: LCSH: Rap (Music)--Political aspects--Egypt. | Rap (Music)--Social
    aspects--Egypt. | Youth--Egypt--Social life and customs--21st century. |
    Egypt--Politics and government--2011-
Classification: LCC ML3917.E3 E57 2023 (print) | LCC ML3917.E3 (ebook) |
    DDC 782.4216490962--dc23/eng/20230314
LC record available at https://lccn.loc.gov/2023011759
LC ebook record available at https://lccn.loc.gov/2023011760

Book design by Strick&Williams
Map design by Jeffrey L. Ward
Author photograph by Brigitte Lacombe

Printed in the United States of America

CONTENTS

Introduction

The modern history of Egypt is told, by insiders and outsiders alike, largely through the narrative of authoritarian leaders and their so-called "iron-fisted" rule. Gamal Abdel Nasser (1956–1970) was well known for his method of having people disappeared—"behind the sun" is the Arabic refrain—if they disagreed with his socialist, nationalist policies, as well as for his persecution of Egypt's Jews. And for thirty years, under the rule of the late Hosni Mubarak (1981–2011), citizens did not dare speak of politics, for fear of the deep state, with its troops of secret police and informants, notorious for their ruthless methods of kidnapping and torture.

This was the atmosphere I grew up in; this was what my parents before me had been raised to understand: politics could put you in jail, if not simply get you vanished away. I learned this myself early on, in the way my parents, their friends, and our relatives distinguished what could or couldn't be said. Rumors were rife about what happened to a classmate's father. We heard snippets of things, but knew we could never ask outright. This, too, was something we came to understand, without ever having to be explicitly told. If we broached a subject that was out of bounds, we were brought to silence, not vocally, but by stern eye contact from an elder. As children, we quickly learned these cues. There were subjects that were never to be addressed.

It was as easy, back then, to control what we spoke of as it was to control what we consumed. There were only two government-operated television channels broadcasting some twelve hours a day, and a third channel that stopped at 1:00 p.m. You were guaranteed to be watching a black-and-white Egyptian film (probably a tragicomic one) twice a day, several newscasts, and an educational program for children, generally about what was morally right and wrong—"never lie to your parents." (The president's wife was referred to on these programs as "Mama" Suzanne.) The greatest indulgence would be a foreign film once every few days (usually a western), and a cartoon (*Tom and Jerry*). This was the universe we were exposed to: a carefully curated worldview courtesy of the Egyptian government's broadcasting arm, a mouthpiece for the Mubarak regime.

Things didn't change much even as Egypt became more exposed in the early 2000s, with the arrival of the internet and eventual widespread access to mobile phones. The government had so successfully indoctrinated citizens—partially through patronage, partially through fear—that few dared to speak out, even if asked to. This undertone of the unspeakable had become so deeply entrenched in the cultural and social fabric of Egypt, that mine was a generation that seemed to simply inherit the silence that our parents had mastered. It was a "know-how," in a sense, that extended fluidly from childhood into early adult-hood. As a journalist working in the country from the age of

12   eighteen, I was quick to learn the "red lines," as we referred to them, the clear parameters of what could or could not be broached. Red lines were considered, tiptoed toward, and never crossed.

The Egyptian Revolution of 2011 changed this atmosphere in fundamental ways, even as its recent ten-year anniversary was marked by a political climate of censorship and human rights abuses. Although official figures are hard to come by, it was estimated by human rights groups that up to 60,000 political dissidents were being held in jail as of late 2022, many for belonging to the wrong political party, or for expressing personal views not aligned with the state.

As I write this, late in 2022, I believe it is fair to say that Egypt is at its most oppressive point in its modern history. Few would contest that. Government and army officials have often been quoted saying that the long-standing "emergency rule" measures have been necessary, to avoid the chaos of Syria, or the political mayhem experienced under the Muslim Brotherhood's rule. The president, Abdel Fattah El-Sisi, has explicitly stated on television that he will never allow what occurred in 2011 to happen again. People I know are in prison simply for voicing opinions or personal experiences. One friend, Alaa Abdel Fattah, a blogger, computer programmer, and activist, was arrested in 2019 for a Facebook post, and has been in prison ever since, on fabricated charges of spreading false news that undermined national security. Freedom of speech is a calculated risk you choose to take.

Yet despite this repressive atmosphere and the constant threat of censorship and silencing, what happened in the eighteen months between January 2011 and July 2013—the street protests that led to the downfall of Mubarak and his clan, and the subsequent ones in 2013 that led to the ouster of Mohamed Morsi, who had become the first freely elected post-revolution president—can perhaps never entirely be reversed. What I am referring to specifically is the breaking of a fear barrier of personal and political expression.

It was a surprise to everyone that the Egyptian Revolution unfurled with the speed and impact that it did, even as there were indications throughout 2010 that something in the political landscape and imagination was shifting—the result of a confluence of predicaments and events. In the span of six months, between the summer and winter of 2010, inflation was at a record high, power cuts had become daily occurrences, and prices of basic commodities skyrocketed. That November, the parliamentary elections were rife with unprecedented thuggery and bullying at the hands of the state, which was angling for Mubarak's son, Gamal (aka Jimmy), to take the helm of the ruling National Democratic Party. He was widely expected to take over from his father, in a succession plan that was being likened to monarchy. Citizen grievances were high. People felt pressured by the inconveniences and economic difficulties of managing the very basic needs of their everyday lives.

On December 31, just weeks before the revolution erupted, a suicide bomber exploded himself outside a church in Alexandria just as worshippers were leaving New Year's Mass, killing twenty-one people. The government was accused by Muslims and Christians alike of neglecting Egypt's minority Coptic community, and a week later, on Coptic Christmas Eve, tens of thousands of Muslims formed human chains around

14 Coptic churches across the country. If suicide bombers intended to blow up the Christians and their churches, they would have to blow up the Muslims first.

Adding to the backdrop of all this were protests raging in nearby Tunisia, which Egyptians watched closely via satellite television. The atmosphere in my home city of Cairo, and across many of the country's twenty-seven other governorates, was tense. You could feel it in the air. On New Year's Day 2011, for the online Egyptian news site, *Ahram Online*, I wrote:

> The cumulative and unprecedented peak of discontent— of the elections, the persecution, and the longstanding economic troubles that plague the majority of the nation's 80 million population—may very well serve to unite disparate groups of activists and politicians, bringing them together in a larger, more forceful movement for change. And the example of Tunisia, and the courage its youth have displayed in risking their lives, may very well be the impetus Egypt's own youth and activists need to take their activities to a new level of vitality.

Less than three weeks later, Egyptians took to the streets of the capital in the tens of thousands, and in cities and towns across the country. I was part of the protest movement from early that morning, when there were just several hundred of us in total marching in different groups through the city's streets. But by late that afternoon, numbers had swelled, and approximately 30,000 protesters had gathered in Tahrir (liberation) Square in central Cairo, in a standoff with riot police that went on for hours. By the time I had left the Square, well after midnight, the crowds were still there, with no signs of leaving—neither the putrid tear gas that filled the air, nor the rubber bullets that were being fired at protesters by the police, had effect. The protesters were steadfast. Three days later, more than a million people joined in a march through Cairo and toward Tahrir Square. From that point on, the numbers simply multiplied by day. Egyptians demonstrated in the streets of the capital, and through cities, towns, and villages across the country, often camping out in public squares in makeshift tents and temporary constructions. They marched with banners calling for reforms and basic rights; they used pots and pans for percussion and drums, and they chanted, mantras such as the most popular refrain, "bread, freedom, social justice." And they broke into song.

Grievances left unspoken for decades had been unleashed, and for eighteen days, Egypt was at a complete standstill. Protests had overrun the country, the internet had been cut off by the government, businesses were shut down, and a curfew was in place from 6:00 p.m. until 7:00 a.m. The army rolled into central Cairo in tanks and trucks, lining main streets and central squares in the name of "protecting the great people" of Egypt. For the most part, however, the officers and soldiers simply stood by, watching. With millions of Egyptians spending nights in the streets, political power—for the first time in decades— lay there. Civilians had taken over patrolling their cities. They were setting the rules of the streets, as well as the political agenda.

In the months that followed, the popular social, political, and economic expression that had found an outlet in the streets in the form of banners and chants extended into the mainstream narrative through articles, websites, magazines, and books. Political parties were formed in unprecedented numbers. Manifestos seemed to be everywhere, posted on lamp-poles, handed out in public squares, and circulated online. Activists founded NGOs and human rights organizations. Critiques of the government, the president, the ministers, and even the long-sacred army became commonplace. The public protest against the government became the go-to means of complaint. Its form became the marching body, and its message in the chants and songs that accompanied it.

Those of us who partook in the "revolution" or "uprising" never expected the sense of agency to end. But it disintegrated when the army formally came to power with the ouster of Morsi in the summer of 2013, and the contrived election the following spring of then—defense minister and army general Abdel Fattah El-Sisi. Muslim Brotherhood members were rounded up by the hundreds and thrown in prison. Politically active citizens were arrested and put through swift trials in military court, without lawyers, bypassing due process, and most of them were thrown in jail. Death sentences became commonplace. A judge sentenced 683 alleged Muslim Brotherhood members to death in a single trial. Gatherings of ten people or more were outlawed. Police began to stop young people in the streets and search their phones. This had never happened before.

Under Mubarak, the political red lines had been clear— black and white, so to speak. Anything critical of the president, his sons, and a small circle of his advisors and confidants— which included businessmen as well as members of parliament and the state—was off limits. One could not address bilateral agreements with Israel, including major trade deals such as the Egypt-Israel gas-supply pipeline. Beyond that, everything was fair game. Under Sisi, those lines morphed, expanding beyond political discourse to include anything from lurid lyrics in a song, to social media posts that are deemed "morally offensive." As I write this, at least six young women are in jail for being in videos said to be in violation of "family principles and values upheld by Egyptian society"—one clip involves a divorcée in tight-fitting clothes dancing with her boyfriend. Such arrests are not a matter of state policy per se, but the Stasi-like practice of "citizen patrolling," of spying, monitoring, and reporting against fellow citizens. This policing system has discouraged anything potentially disruptive to the state, to include content posted by local social media influencers.

The content is perhaps less the offense than is the number of viewers who see it; under a law passed in 2018, social media users with more than 5,000 followers are considered "media outlets," making them subject to prosecution for publishing anything considered "false news" or "incitement"—umbrella terms that can be twisted to include most all personal expression. In a state that has deemed itself perennially at threat, there are also no clear-cut criterion—the only constant is that parameters are continually shifting. Who is reported, prosecuted, arrested, released—all this is arbitrary.

Within this political climate, it is telling, then, that Egypt's independent music scene, with its Arabic genre of hip-hop, known as *mahraganat*, has been thriving. In the tradition of Snoop Dogg, Tupac, Eminem, and Jay-Z, and borrowing from the history and technical forms of the genre, these Egyptian

18   music artists are reliant on lyrics grounded in deeply personal, political, sexual, and socioeconomic realities—most everything the government would prefer citizens not to speak about, and the kind of material that citizen patrols love to report. The artists rap about their own lives, their neighborhoods, their rivals, their personal, economic, and political battles, as well as their successes, money, women, and dreams. In one song, for example, the duo Oka and Ortega rhapsodized about drinking alcohol and taking drugs—both considered blasphemy in Islam, and the drugs, needless to say, punishable with jail:

> You're sitting alone, idle-minded
> Satan is leading you to the wrong path
> He keeps telling you "let's play, dude"
> Let's play, dude, why don't you play, dude, let's play, dude,
>   let's play, dude
>
> You want to be a man of principle
> quit the drugs
> and say "I'm starting"
> Satan comes and keeps telling you
> Drink, dude, drink, dude, light it, dude

A growing league of local artists, mostly in their twenties, boast millions of followers online. They have sold-out concerts at licensed venues, but also at street weddings and private parties, even as the state has repeatedly attempted to shut them down. Many of the most popular of these music artists were too young to properly partake in the Egyptian Revolution—most of them were pre-teens or in their early teens—but they came of age at that moment of rupture, when everyone was speaking out. It has, over time, come to define who they are, too—outspoken, uninhibited, independent, *free*.

Unlike my generation, which came of age in the nineties and was raised in constant fear of speech, the rules of the game for these music hipsters don't abide by any social or cultural norms the country has known before. The long-held parameters of what can and can't be said have become obsolete in their hands. They rap about long-taboo issues. They have no hesitations, and political fears seem not to exist for them.

These singers have commanded my attention, even envy at first, precisely for their lack of inhibition—for their fierce assertion of independent, nonconformist identities. They are free in an environment that does everything it can to break individual freedoms. They did not cave in, as my generational peers did. They do not swallow their words.

Egypt's official population is pushing 105 million citizens. It is widely known that the number is larger—some analysts estimate by at least 5 to 7 percent. In August 2022, the government announced that the population had grown by 750,000 in the past six months. Sixty percent of that population, or 65 million people, are under the age of twenty-nine, so it is no surprise that these young musicians have millions of fans at their command. It is those fans, influenced by the music artists they revere, who are the future of the country—the ones who will essentially define what Egypt comes to be.

In as much as one can attempt to capture the energy and dynamics of a place as vast and diverse as Egypt, this book is a distillation of an ongoing moment in time, through the prism of

20   a segment of these youth, and with a view to the future. The artists profiled are all illustrative, but they are also select—there
are at least one hundred more that make up the scene. This book
is not written for the insider, neither of the music scene nor of
the country. Many of us who live here know this history and
these stories, albeit through divergent political viewpoints and
proximities. The book is therefore intended for the millions
who had followed the Egyptian Revolution with intrigue, and
have since turned their attention elsewhere. The story of Egypt,
and of its revolutionary fervor, is not yet over.

Marwan Pablo

A three-hour drive north of Cairo, across the desert and cutting through a western sliver of the Nile Delta, lies the ancient port city of Alexandria. Founded in 331 BC by Alexander the Great, it eventually became the seat of the Ptolemaic Kingdom, a place known for learning, innovation, and knowledge, second only to Rome in wealth, cultural riches, and power. Over centuries and under different rulers ending with the British Occupation, Alexandria remained a haven for artists, writers, and foreign visitors.

That ended, somewhat abruptly, with the military ouster of King Farouk in 1952 from his summer palace in Alexandria. Pushed out by Nasser and the Free Officers, Farouk departed Egypt straight from the city's shores to Italy, where he eventually died in exile. In his place, Nasser championed a brand of nationalism that persecuted the wealthy and pushed out the Jews, the Italians, and the Greeks. This ruptured the very cosmopolitism of Alexandria, ushering in a new, conservative milieu. Under Mubarak, notoriously repressive state security

22   agents had ruthlessly run the Islamists underground. But when the revolution erupted in 2011, leading to Mubarak's ouster, the underbelly of Alexandria emerged: it was the cradle of Salafism, one of Islam's most conservative branches. The streets began to transform visually. They became populated with women covered entirely in black robes, with only their eyes showing. Beside them were men with bushy, unkempt beards, dressed in traditional *galabiyas* worn short, just above the ankle. Among liberals, the city came to be referred to as "Salafiland." It was also run-down, overbuilt, and falling into decay. It was hard not to take note that the Alexandria many of our parents had known— of beaches filled with nearly bare bodies, a haven for literature, music, and art—was no more.

What Alexandria was, and what it had become—the contrast of those two realities and the pressure it created on young people to be one extreme or the other—shaped the artists who called the city home. A big part of cultural revival efforts was the 2002 inauguration of the modern Bibliothecha Alexandrina, a commemoration of the Great Library of Alexandria, which had been built during the Ptolemic period as one of the most significant libraries of the ancient world. "It's a place still of the imagination; what remains of long and varied historic rules is omnipresent, inescapable," curator Sarah Rifky said at a lecture there in 2012. The old Alexandria still existed to inspire, in the wide boulevards, art deco buildings, the Musee des Beaux-Arts, and the intricate and ornate architecture that lines the Corniche. The remains of the deposed king's former summer palace frame one end of the coastline. On the other end stands the fifteenth-century citadel of Qaitbay, the architecture of a different kind of power and preoccupation. Somewhere between these spots was the villa where Lawrence Durrell lived, the backdrop to the Alexandria Quartet; and nearby are the ruins of the fourth-century Roman Amphitheatre. Buried beneath the coast somewhere under all this lies the historic library. Within this storied context, Alexandria had nurtured some of Egypt's most prominent artists, including the Greek-Egyptian poet C. P. Cavafy, whose lifelong apartment still remains as he once inhabited it, now a museum and currently under restoration. And yet burgeoning all around was an Islamist political agenda and way of life.

This fraught contemporary context was the pull for the influential international exhibition Documenta to hold a portion of its thirteenth edition in the city in the summer of 2012, coincidentally just days after the country voted a Muslim Brotherhood member to power as president. This was the setting for Rifky's talk, as two dozen of the most prominent contemporary musicians, artists, filmmakers, thinkers, and curators traveled from around the world to draw inspiration from the city. Contrary to its historic peers, Alexandria had moved in what was perceived as opposition to common notions of "progress," turning toward conservative ideals, demolishing as much of the old architecture as possible, crowding out the coastline with modern brutalist structures. It was no longer a place you would feel comfortable wearing a bathing suit at a public beach. The revolution called for freedom and brought new elections—but the people voted in political Islam. With the results just in, this was all the artists could discuss. Although this appeared to be the direction Egypt was taking with the emergence of the Muslim Brotherhood, nowhere was it more acutely felt than in Alexandria.

It is those contradictions, and the pressures of extremities— to be one way or another, to exist between worlds—that some of

24   the city's young rappers refer to as their molding. These contradictions serve as a notional backdrop to understand the music scene as a whole: Alexandria is the unlikely case study and reference point for the personalities, and political, cultural, and economic contexts and concerns, of a generation now speaking out. These are the tail ends of a national spectrum of circumstances. When they were being pushed to one extreme, young people often emerged on the other end.

Marwan Pablo, first known as Dama, and then as Pablo, was born as Marwan Ahmed Mutaw'a. He is a committed Alexandrian, and one of Egypt's most popular and successful young rappers—or "trappers." Although most artists use these terms interchangeably, "trap" is formally defined by synthesized, multilayered beats to the backdrop of lyrics. It denotes a different level of technical expertise.

Like his peers, Pablo grew up well aware of his city's history. The Alexandrian neighborhood he called home, El-Hadra, is a dense place set in from the shoreline, with both housing projects and buildings that are unfinished, where windows face other windows. The streets are mostly narrow, and workshops and warehouses line one side of an outer road leading into the area—a demarcation between the different Alexandrias. Pablo's is the one that emerged out of Nasser's Egypt and grew under Mubarak's, as the population boomed and housing was built at low cost, both by the government and also by citizens trying to provide shelter for themselves. It is a type of neighborhood that is replicated nationwide.

In his early teens, Pablo began to hang out at the internet cafés that had opened in the neighborhood, renting out internet time in ten-minute slots. Mostly he listened to tunes and music

videos online. "You ask me where it came from, the inspiration,"
he said. "I don't know. But I was thirteen or fourteen when,
bam!, lyrics came to me atop a beat." Pablo's means were primi-
tive. He started to upload his blend of lyrics to beats, recorded
on outdated computers, onto already existing tracks. At first it
was two tracks in a day, hasty recordings put together without
much thought. He would spend five minutes thinking about a
beat, and fifteen minutes writing the words. "I was working on
instinct but also didn't know exactly what I was doing," he said.
"I'd then go hang out in the streets with friends for a few days
and then come back and write everything that happened. That
was a track."

Pablo was writing his own lyrics without anyone's help,
which was unusual. "Nobody can write," he said. In Egyptian
hip-hop, writing is usually a group effort—a gathering of
friends and colleagues bouncing around ideas or borrowing
from one another. Pablo credits the skill to write on his own to
his parents, who he describes as of limited means but rich of
mind. They understood education was key, and with what
resources they had, enrolled him in a language school. "A language school is a happy place. Life is good and the kids are happy
and it's co-ed. It's in a good part of the city. Then my neighborhood is very conservative, and poor. There was a vast gap in
thinking and culture. So I was low-class for the language school
kids and a soft sellout for my neighborhood community. This
creates a divide."

When Nasser had come to power, he overhauled the education system and made access to schools free. The population
was small, and the country could afford to subsidize learning,
extending it even to Arab and African citizens, and still pay

26 teachers well. The public school system was the nation's pride. But the economic tolls of war, coupled with the population explosion, meant resources came to be spread thin. Schools multiplied, teacher salaries declined relative to the cost of living. The drop in the quality of learning was steep. Today, and for the past forty years, the neglect of the education system has widely been thought to be intentional—a matter of state policy, to keep the population ignorant, quiet, and at bay. Teachers are grossly underpaid, disengaged, and seldom show up. Education in the actual classroom is nonexistent, unless you can afford private lessons, which few can. Children speak a street vernacular, but lack basic command of "proper" Arabic—the type used at high levels of government, media, and business. It is a generation that in some sense has been muted. Most of Pablo's peers came out of that public school system. But even Pablo himself, who *can* write, doesn't speak in full or clear sentences. One in every three of his words is an interjection: *nikh* or *fashkh* usually, the slang for *totally* and *awesome*, but in Arabic both words also hold crude undertones.

In 2015, Pablo, then twenty-two, created the stage name Dama, which comes from the word for the game "checkers." As Dama, he uploaded a series of songs about falling in love, heartbreak, money, and freedom. The music was like heavy metal toned down a couple of notches. The words were raw, too. In his most known song from the time, "One Copy," he rapped about his limited means, and forgetting a girl by drinking: "To forget / What do you need to forget / Drink this to forget / Not because of this you forget / The dirtiest lie, for you / And she, will drink this to forget, for you to forget / And for what, to break you /

You're going to have to break me to win." Midway through that song, he veered into English, borrowed from American rap: "Shit lame niggaz can't relate to me / Never give a fuck / Never trust a bitch, yeah / Unfortunately just One Copy / There is not / Another man."

He wasn't the first one to reference alcohol or to use swear words, but for such a little-known artist, it was risky—in a culture where alcohol is forbidden by religion, his lyrics could have been widely shunned by the conservative community around him in Alexandria. If he didn't rise to fame, these lyrics could have come to be his downfall.

At the time, Dama had only a small audience among the neighborhood kids. "That was the scene, literally a small circle of people around you on the street," he said. Cairo, the capital, was the place you had to be to make music and money. To have fans, you had to go south. "When I was growing up, there were no venues in Alexandria for new and cool music," he said. "Everything was telling me go to Cairo. But I didn't want it that way. I wanted the people in Cairo to feel that Alexandria is where it's all happening, where they had to come. I didn't want Alexandria to be weak in the way it was."

Although he was making and uploading music consistently, things were slow-moving. He came to understand that the only way to elevate himself, and Alexandria, was by trying to raise rap to a new level. In 2017, despite having a small but solid circle of fans and watching critics, he decided to metaphorically "kill Dama," by going completely underground. For a whole year, there was no sign of him. No Dama and no Marwan. He had all but been erased online. No social media accounts, no

28   profiles on any music channels, and with the exception of songs that had been archived by others, Dama may well have never existed. In interviews from soon after he reemerged, he was criticized for abandoning his fans. He dismissed it as for the greater good of rap. "That person technically died," he explained to a music critic. "I killed him. And now there's me, Marwan Pablo. Everything is new. Technically, lyrics, me, look at me. This is me. Marwan Pablo." In place of Dama, he had created another character—Marwan Pablo, a reference to both Pablo Escobar and Pablo Picasso.

The song that Marwan Pablo (aka Pablo) came out with in his rebirth, "El Gholaf X Ozoris" (*el gholaf* means "the cover"), soared in the charts and began to bring him the kind of attention he had hoped for. It was technically more proficient, with unique beats and sounds, and more carefully thought and felt lyrics:

> I wanted, once, to find myself
> I broke a tooth, and in the place of it came a fang
> What you've seen of me is just the cover
> It's hard for me to open the book for you
> It's easy for me to blow open your mind
> I'm sorry the dispute will end
> I'm sorry the dispute will end
> I'm sorry the dispute will end
> My God he told me not to become an icon
> To never lose sight of me and go to others for refuge
> None of them will hear you
> No matter how much you call or how much you shout
> We are different, and all envious eyes are on us

Our path is clear, so up we rise
In the end, are two types of people in this world
Those who rust, and those who shine
A working mind does not rest

Pablo was digging deeper, emotionally, than anything in the genre at the time. He was also asserting identity and individual values, the kinds of thoughts being curtailed by the culture and religion that was ascendant in Alexandria. In conversations, he alluded to experiencing depression at that time. "Where am I going, how does it end, stuff like that, these thoughts used to paralyze me, but I stopped thinking that way," he said. "This is not just about music. It's much broader, about life."

Pablo was young when the revolution erupted, but old enough to know what it promised for the lives of people like himself. For the eighteen days that Egyptians had been camped out in squares across the country, it was clear that the majority of the youth were there for the promise of better lives, better homes, better neighborhoods. They chanted songs and slogans to this effect, and in crude rap-styled bursts of chanting, talked about having the desire to marry, but not the means. Essentially, the revolution was the promise of resources (like jobs) that would enable them to get the apartments and furnishings necessary to be "marriageable" (culturally suitable as grooms). They were promises that had essentially dissipated by 2015, when a witch hunt by the government against the Islamists had also reached its peak. Between 2013 and 2015, in neighborhoods across Alexandria as well as other governorates, police vehicles with masked special forces stormed buildings,

30   kicked down apartment doors, dragged out men and, on occasion, women, and took them away. Crackdowns were violent and extreme, and these incidents were rampant.

It was not easy to be a young man, and certainly not one from the working class or from a conservative neighborhood. The threat of being persecuted by the state was constant, and decent jobs were hard to come by. Pablo himself worked several jobs, enough to make a basic living. He began at Carrefour, the French-Egyptian equivalent of America's Target, first in the men's clothing section, before getting into a disagreement with a customer and being moved to the children's department. All the time, he was writing music. "This wasn't an easy field to start in, not because of talent or success but because of societal and family pressures. You want to get married. What are you going to tell your bride's family, that you sing rap?" he said. "This depression you go through, the thoughts you get, are connected to this place. You stay here thinking about these problems in this place—they become one. If you're looking for inspiration, you're not going to find it. Up until recently I was not sure what I was going to do—university or what—where I would end up. Then I made 'El Gholaf.' With that, I found my path and understood that this is my destiny. That's my signature. I killed Dama and came back stronger."

"El Gholaf X Ozoris" was followed quickly by what might be considered his solo breakout, "Sindbad." Its lyrics were catchy and different:

> *Bitch* I'm in the zone
> Leave the past behind
> Wanna give me runarounds

Go date Sindbad
I don't see you in my future I won't lie
Envy me all you want
You won't get under my skin
I feel like I'm the best one who ever did it (yeah, yeah, yeah)
A new year and you're still fixed in my mind like the
     Mona Lisa
Good morning
Had no sleep since yesterday
All night staring at the sky
Sounds cliche, I know
But *really*
A year that smells like money
Smells like alcohol, smells like lessons
It went fine, I'm not in jail
Thank God

"Sindbad" brought Pablo gigs. Everyone could understand his plain language and his talk of money. But the song was also highly political, even as it steered clear of direct political commentary. "Sindbad" had echoes of Jay-Z rapping as a Black man still being subjected to racism, but in the case of Pablo and Egypt, Blackness was replaced by class. The government's repressive security apparatus had always persecuted young, poor men, framing them, using them as scapegoats, and simply keeping the population fearful by being ruthless as a matter of messaging and policy. "Sindbad" was rising above the circumstances that plagued young men like himself, to buy himself freedom. The leading Cairene *mahraganat* producers took an interest. A series of songs followed, in addition to an appearance in an Arabic

32   documentary on the genre. His collaborations with the Cairo-based producer Molotof (after the Molotov cocktails that were used by young protesters during the 2011 revolution) were the cornerstones for what would become his rise in the charts.

Pablo's most popular track at the time was "Free," a song that became something of an anthem for the freeing of the mind through a state-of-consciousness that can only come under the influence of drugs ("If you go crazy then you are free / We drive the world to Mars / We drive the world with no benzine / If you go crazy then you are free"), and it was beginning to be streamed millions of times online. Young people driving *tok-toks,* or three-wheeled taxis, started playing Pablo's song from thumb drives, which was the ultimate measure of fame. The song was a breakthrough in terms of reach, and the government took note. The most threatening phenomenon to the state has always been any single force with the power to attract crowds, which in turn could mean the mobilization of masses. It would be a convenient foil that the song encouraged drug-taking should the authorities decide to use it as the pretense for a crackdown, but for Pablo, these songs were calculated and considered in that way.

The video for the song was shot in Alexandria. It featured atmospheric cinematography of the city: Pablo in a car, at a graveyard, on the corniche, smoking, singing, dancing, and drinking. Together with Molotof, they roam the city that nurtured the creativity that set him "free." Pablo both critiqued the country's suffocating circumstances and touted the liberation that came with mind-altering substances. Soon after, he released another track, "Geb Felos," or "Get Money," like the 1995 song by the Notorious B.I.G. It runs in loops, and is about the catch-22 of wealth:

My friend, get me money, get me money
I went to a Sheikh, he said I'm cursed
I'm trapped here, I'm trapped
The Sheikh said, give me money
My devil tells me, get me money, get me money
People say
Give me money, give me money

Songs like "Free" and "Geb Felos" made Pablo one of the most popular trap artists across both Alexandria and Cairo. His lyrics tackled problems of daily life (a lack of money) and the only means of escaping it (drugs). He also had no fear of what people might think, of cultural taboos, or of how the government or the ultra-conservative and religiously inclined community around him might respond. But as his listener ranks climbed, giving *mahraganat* a broader reach, people began to talk about cultural values changing, even being broken. Something was shifting.

In 2020, on the back of his stratospheric rise, Marwan Pablo suddenly announced that he was retiring, again, at the young age of twenty-four. He wouldn't speak or give interviews about it, but in a statement that he circulated via Instagram, he made the announcement, saying, "Please, nobody ask me to return. I am now in the service of God, and I am hoping that God will be accepting of this, of me. And for anyone hearing me and believing me, what you can offer is prayers that God accepts and forgives and blesses me."

Whether the second disappearance was a media or technical ploy, Marwan Pablo has refused to say, but when he reemerged in 2021, it could well have been a metaphorical killing of the old Pablo for the birthing of a new, more technically proficient one.

34   He came back with "Ghaba" ("The Jungle"), a song that amassed
1.9 million views in the first few hours of its release, and had hit
23.5 million views within a few weeks of its release. It made it to
the Egyptian charts, spending sixty-seven weeks at the top
spot. Critics started to refer to him as the "Godfather of Trap,"
and in an advertisement for the mobile phone carrier Vodafone,
one of only three providers in the country, the campaign brief
prepared by the advertising firm Wunderman Thompson/JWT
for the client describes the campaign and Marwan Pablo in these
terms:

> Inspiration: Similar to rappers across the world, rappers in
> Egypt take to battles and beefs, and crowning the one with
> the best flow, style, and lyrics. Yet the major question was,
> who could complete with the number one rapper in Egypt,
> while remaining a fair fight? While the question was ambi-
> tious, it left only one choice; that only Marwan Pablo can
> battle Marwan Pablo, because, if there aren't any like you,
> then you can only compete with yourself alone.

The Egyptian mobile carrier network is made up of approximately 96 million subscribers, of which 40 million use
Vodafone. Pablo was being thought of and positioned as a
national influencer. An advertisement for the network meant a
nationwide audience, but with that would come the scruti-
nizing eye of the government.

3enaabb aka 3enba

3enba
Performing live, 7:00 p.m.
Doors open 4:00 p.m., close at 7:00 p.m.
No phones,
No cameras,
No drinks,
No alcohol,
No firecrackers,
No fire-making devices,
No perfume bottles,
No media,
No banners.

This was the wording of the flyer that circulated across social media in the days leading up to February 1, 2022. On social media groups for local outings and events, discussions were feverish around the rules. Those attending wanted their phones, cameras, and drinks. Those not attending wanted to know what

36   the organizers were anticipating with such stringent rules. (The flyer was forwarded to me a dozen times in different and unrelated WhatsApp groups.) What were they hiding by banning phones and cameras? What was expected? 3enba was among the music artists at the forefront of a once-fringe genre of music now filtering into the mainstream. He was following the path of his better-known peers such as Marwan Pablo, Mohamed Ramadan, Oka and Ortega, and Hassan Shakosh, and they were ruffling societal feathers. On one Facebook group for local arts and culture events and news, a lawyer posted the 3enba flyer and suggested bringing a case against such concerts, saying that they are "disruptive to our culture." Such a case would fall under one of Egypt's several ambiguously worded laws that criminalize anything that could be argued to be "debauchery," "blasphemy," or "infringing on family values."

On February 1, approximately five hundred young men filled the streets around the open-air theater from early in the day in anticipation of 3enba. His name means "the grape," and the "3" is used to fill in for a soft-A that exists in Arabic; linguists describe the sound as "voiced pharyngeal fricative." He had been livestreaming chats with his fans for days on social media platforms like Instagram (where he has 2 million followers, and growing), doing little but posing and showing off outfits, in a black sports car and what seemed to be luxury hotel rooms. His concert was sold out, and fans were begging him for more dates, more tickets, more livestream chats, more everything. "We want more grapes," one fan shouted into a livestream chat that 3enba shared with viewers.

A few days before the concert, 3enba had appeared on-air via a phone-in with Amr Adib, one of Egypt's most popular talk show hosts, and an unapologetic government mouthpiece. He had been invited onto the show to announce to his fans the news that he had passed the Egyptian Musicians Syndicate's licensing test and procedures. This made him "legal to perform." It was also a vote of confidence. The Syndicate is an officiating entity that "validates" performers who have to undergo an audition by committee. To be syndicated implies a certain "standard," "quality," and "professionalism." It even comes with benefits, like healthcare and government-related discounts, on the country's official airline carrier, EgyptAir, for example. But in a country with a heavy hand on any medium/event/action that has the potential for widespread appeal and following, syndication is a double-edged sword. While prestige and benefits count for something, the Syndicate is also a censorship arm of the government. To be syndicated binds you, to some extent, to conform. This is true not just of musicians, but across mainstream media, such as newspapers. Although performing (or publishing) is technically still possible without being a member of the relevant Syndicate, it comes with its own risk of fines, or possibly imprisonment. Plainclothes Syndicate "informers" have been known to frequent cabaret venues and performance spaces to catch non-licensed performers "in the act."

For 3enba, syndication was a coup. The Syndicate has historically licensed only mainstream performers, and played a significant role in cracking down on new, more Western-inclined genres. Heavy metal concerts were banned and cast as "devil-worshipping" in the nineties, resulting in arrests and imprisonments. More recently, during a concert in the United Arab Emirates just before the pandemic, a fan requested that popular Egyptian singer Sherine Abdel Wahab sing her hit song

38   "Ma'shiribteesh min Nilha" ("Haven't You Drunk from Her Nile"), but the singer responded jokingly, "No, you'd get Schistosomiasis [a waterborne parasitic disease]. Drink Evian, it's better!" The video of the incident went viral, and then-Syndicate president Hani Shaker, a famous pop singer himself from the nineties, banned Sherine from performing in Egypt, and publicly supported an arrest warrant against her for "insulting Egypt."

On-air with Amr Adib, 3enba was jittery. He asked if the interview was also part of the Syndicate's "test" to allow him to perform. "Is this still part of the process or am I approved already?" he said. "Just tell me." He was even nudged to explain his lyrics. "It's just *fet'a*, the food," he said of one question, referring to a traditional dish of bread, rice, and lamb. "Really just food, not some other meaning that is bad." He also explained that "mob" doesn't refer to gangs. "Mob doesn't always mean something bad, it's just another way of saying guys, like, you know, at the street corner or something like that," he said. "No guns." 3enba also shared that he was slightly altering his name to 3enaabb, the name of a juice drink.

3enaabb's performer license was issued for a term of one year, and he quickly started to take bookings. His fan base was growing, and they showed up to the February concert wearing knockoffs of Valentino, Gucci, Balenciaga, Yves Saint Laurent, and Moncler. They sported fake gold chunky chains. Their hairstyles comprised an array of blow-dried, slick, carefully coiffed dos. They had mostly walked from poorer neighborhoods to an open-air theater housed on the grounds of a members-only urban sports and social club for officers of the armed forces and their families. Outside, as they waited for doors to open, they posed for photographs, bought sandwiches, coffees, and soft drinks from little shacks nearby, and simply strutted the streets, conscious of being dressed to impress. Young photographers with light-rings offered "professional" social-media-ready shots for less than one US dollar. "Fame isn't always about having a good voice," one young man said, but rather, "it's just about looking the part." This "looking the part" is called "famous"—the English word itself is used, even among youth who otherwise don't speak a word of it. Essentially, *famous* is a trend of young men with elaborate and gravity-defying hairstyles who post professionally shot portraits of themselves online. The goal is to attract as many social media followers as a famous singer, since social media fame leads to money. Some also hope that someone will cast them as extras in music videos or on TV.

3enaabb, who is in his mid-twenties, grew up in a poor neighborhood in the center of historic Cairo known as Herafiyeen, which means "craft workers," or "craftspeople who work with their hands." It's an area best known for its metal workshops, for the finely chiseled brass and copper decorative wares made there. His real name is Mostafa, and as a young boy in school, he made up tunes in his head constantly. "If you listened closely, I was always humming things to myself," he said. These childhood beats are what eventually set him apart. "My lyrics make me real—it's something felt. I'm writing and singing about my own experiences, even though I sing in one song about dealing drugs, but I've never sold drugs."

The song he refers to is his breakout, "Ibn Al-Balad," or "Son of the Country," a slang turn of phrase meaning someone of the land and the Nile. The lyrics riff on the economic hardship of life and the lack of direction of the people around him:

40
I've come my country
Not in mass, not in numbers
(not in numbers, not in numbers)
Deadbeats around in abundance
(Abundance, I say, abundance, abundance)
Good-for-nothings, there is no hope
(Go hard)
Get away from me, my nerves are tired
You addict kids, drowning
We're a nation against destruction
You want to try, come over
If you come over here, here will be ripped up
I'm as great as any square
I steer with my heart, I am a street
Like benzine, I ignite

Recorded on a track by Molotof, he made the single on a whim. "We recorded, uploaded, and bam." The video was an equally quick affair, filmed in his neighborhood by Diablo, a now-famous music-video director, with a borrowed camera, wearing "just the black t-shirts we each had." The video became immensely popular, precisely because of this low-fi, low-budget, no-pretenses approach. He spoke of circumstances everyone could relate to, in a setting that looked like the alley where anyone of his audience might live. There was no acting like things were easy. There was no glamour, no girls, no machismo or showing off, even as he addressed the desire and tendency to be that way. This was, and remains, his appeal.

3enaabb serves as a good reference to understand his demographic and the new generational landscape: the young men who make up the bulk of the country's population. The median age in Egypt is 24.6 years old, and men outnumber women. Approximately 40 percent of the population live in informally planned areas that are themselves extensions of the most densely populated, and oldest, parts of the city. Their families, for the most part, are just getting by. 3enaabb ticks all these boxes. Even the way he talks serves as a guide; the break away from conventional vernacular norms. Everything is slang—a deep-street new-generation slang with its own idioms. Full sentences are few and far between. Everyone has a nickname, like *sawareekh* (rocket), *gusbara* (coriander), and Nigeria. His social media followers (they still call him 3enba) have climbed steadily by tens of thousands a month, because he, like Marwan Pablo, speaks from his own experience, as a twenty-something who has grown up in a neighborhood that represents the kind of place where the majority of Egyptians live. He doesn't try to "spice things up," "American style," like many other artists.

"America is the greatest influence of everyone," 3enaabb explained. "You ask me who inspires me most, who I get ideas from, who I borrow tracks from, who I would want to sing with. Will Smith." 3enaabb is appropriately well versed on different aspects of Americana, including Will Smith, the Bronx, and Compton, the Southern California city that was the birthplace of Dr. Dre, Kendrick Lamar, Lil' Nation, Eazy-E, and others. "Everyone knows I borrowed a Will Smith track and made it Egyptian. It's not wrong. He's famous, I don't hide that it's his track." The recording "Party Starter X Tayarat" fused the two songs to synthesized Arabic beats. In the YouTube comments section of the music video, many of his fans address Will Smith directly, writing: "Your song is now Egyptian, Man!"

Many *mahraganat* songs riff on power over girls, but not 3enaabb. "Everyone asks why I don't write to impress, but I just can't do it." Instead, he is drawn to writing mostly "about the life of youth like myself." Those lives are essentially a political commentary, about the government and its failures— the gap between the hopes and wishes of a generation, and the realities of what the country affords them. What is remarkable in all this, and in what 3enaabb and his peers represent, is the fact that it is the first time in decades that the disenfranchised youth of the country have a voice that speaks for them, like an ethnographic study served up publicly for the world to read. These have been the voices, the stories, the conditions that the government had so fiercely worked to suppress, both up until the revolution, and then with the crackdown that began in 2013.

In the early months of the pandemic, Egypt was under a strict daytime lockdown, and cafés, restaurants, and even the informal and tucked-away local coffee and *shisha* (hookah) joints were closed. This was unusual for a country where previous curfews were disregarded. But this time, young people mostly stayed at home, at most walking the streets for air in the hours before the 5:00 p.m. curfew. There was nothing to do except walk, and once the curfew struck, the only escape from the house was to look out the window of your apartment block, sit on a balcony if you were lucky enough to have one, or go up to the roof of your building. For many Egyptians, this was the only access to space, and an open horizon. 3enaabb was no exception. "I looked up at the sky one day during the lockdown, no one had anywhere to go, and the sky was just filled with kites." From rooftops around

the city in poorer neighborhoods, young children and adults
alike were flying homemade kites. Everyone saw it, from every
neighborhood. Kites constructed of paper, sheet plastic, and
light bamboo cane—the type that had marked childhoods
before the advent of smartphones—were suddenly back, dot-
ting the skyline.

His song "Tayarat," which means both "kites" and "cur-
rents," is about how during COVID "the current has changed
and it's all about kites." In the music video, he and his crew try
to fly a handmade four-meter kite. The wind blows it against a
building, where it gets stuck. The single was an instant hit, as was
the video. One started to hear it stream even at the Starbucks in
more upscale neighborhoods. This seemed to be a good example
of how a genre might propel itself into the mainstream—by
becoming as much a commentary for the youth and their trou-
bles as it was a marker of shared time. This was the kind of
music that the Syndicate liked. His was a different kind of popular power. Another hit, also released shortly after COVID, "El
Melouk," or "The Kings," was featured in an episode of the
Marvel TV show *Moon Knight*. The song is a collaboration with
the rappers Ahmed Saad and Double Zukksh. Unlike his solo
singles, which are predominantly personal and nuanced, his
features with others have an edge of machismo, riffing about
fame and talking about money and success.

As the pandemic started to shake itself off, and life returned
to normal, artists and influencers returned to traveling and
posting online again. To keep up, 3enaabb also focused more
on his online persona and music videos. He began to wear
silky shirts and shorts with Gucci and Chanel logos, with wads
of Egyptian pounds and US dollars scattered around him in

44   photographs. In one post he hung out around a pool at a villa with his friends, posing for another shot in chunky gold chains and black Balenciaga sunglasses. It's hard to reconcile the singer pondering about kites and the tides of change and this designer-clad persona with piles of dollar bills; might the thoughtful, reflective artist in him eventually yield to external pressures?

Some critics even wonder if his syndication was a ploy by the authorities to use an eager, up-and-coming, somewhat "well-behaved" artist to cast themselves as supportive of young musicians. It would be hard to properly call out the government for censorship and cracking down on artists with the popular 3enaabb on-air, talking to the country's most influential TV talk show host. On a recent trip to the UAE to perform, he posted on his Instagram live-feed a photo of himself as he was shown into his sprawling luxurious hotel suite. On the photo he had handwritten, in Arabic, the words: "Egypt, Mother of the World." Because 3enaabb had arrived on the scene, so had the country that had syndicated him.

Diss

Hip-hop is famous for the "diss," a track conceived on the back of a borrowing or appropriation of lyrics, ungiven credit, political positions, or simply machismo. It's a matter of pride, and form. Sometimes these battles are riffs based on singles released to the public—one song followed by another in answer. But a rap battle can also be an organized and orchestrated event, often in dingy quarters, on the streets, or at more widely attended rap-battle festivals. These are a display of technical skill and ingenuity. When released in the form of tracks in reply to another's song, these back-and-forth numbers of inventive narrative and lyrics can go on for years. Sales are built on these duels, with fans eagerly awaiting the responding singles to be released. The diss is a vast platform for growth—of individual music artists, as well as the form as a whole.

In Egypt, it was the low-fi, street-based, underground diss battle that was the initial growth channel. It was 2016, *mahraganat* was finding traction, and the street was the surest way to begin to gather fans and fame, especially for wannabe artists

46   without the means to record. Spontaneous gatherings were popping up across Cairo and Alexandria—aspiring rappers testing their skill to small neighborhood crowds. One street battle that is often cited as a public birthstone for the local *diss* (perhaps because its videography was choreographed with the target of an online audience) is one that took place between 3atwa and Yousef Joker, to a crowd of some three hundred young men. It was a raw back-and-forth, taking jabs at image, persona, and the artist in the making: who bows down to whom, how low one stoops for fame, what one wears, how one spends days, and to whom does one listen for inspiration—Will Smith (again) versus the Egyptian movie star Faten Hamama (known for her romantic dramas). The gathered cheerers-on were all from similar socioeconomic circumstances to those rapping—mainly working class. Many of them had grown up in housing projects or informally planned settlements, in households where everyone had to earn their own share of the family's living. The voice of that life—this underclass—was essentially the birth of the genre.

The diss has played a part in propelling some of the genre's local elite to wider, more diverse audiences. Among them, the now international breakout sensation Wegz, who went on to perform at the closing ceremony of the 2022 World Cup in Qatar, and the former metal musician Abyusif, who has always been something of an anomaly to the scene by way of his class background, but has also reached the charts' top ranks.

Abyusif was raised on an upscale residential island with wide, paved, tree-lined streets; a place with buildings that look like they might have been lifted from Europe (many were, in fact, built under occupation). The neighborhood, Zamalek, is where the foreign embassies reside, housed in villas that were previously parts of palaces or the homes of the country's now fallen and departed aristocracy—a lineage that still marks the island's reputation, even as it is subject to change at the hands of a new government intent on breaking down previous orders of class, privilege, and connections. Zamalek is ten minutes away from Tahrir Square, but politically worlds apart—during the revolution, a significant chunk of the island's residents were labeled "hezb el kanaba," or "the party of the couch," for not participating.

In short, the rapper was born to privilege, as Youssef Mohamed Altay. The son of a jazz drummer, he was first part of a metal band called The Overlord of the Brewing Women (their music has been described as Pink Floyd meets rap) before venturing into hip-hop, where he steered his own path in the genre. After the 2011 uprising, when everyone was writing, singing, and making films and art tied to the political narrative, Abyusif was singing about pop culture, its influence, the process of making music, and what it means to be young. It seemed like he had a sort of old-school foresight, about the problems of political positions: "They change," he has explained. "Songs become irrelevant as political positions evolve." Inasmuch as Abyusif's lyrics were inventive, and fervent, they struck a mismatched chord with fans from different socioeconomic backgrounds, those whose preoccupations revolved around commonplace issues such as having enough money for a bus ticket, or being able to top up phone credit. In some sense, his was the music of privilege—not just what he chose to rap about, but very much what he steered away from. No religion ("That's between the individual and their God"). No derogatory lyrics about women

48 ("I prefer to think of them as equals"). But Abyusif's rate of releasing singles was consistent, even prolific—he was impossible to shrug off. He had been around long enough to become a contender among fellow rappers—they followed him as a peer, even if his fan base didn't touch the masses.

That reach changed when Abyusif and a trapper by the name of Wegz went head-to-head in a diss battle. Wegz (his childhood nickname by a friend) was born as Ahmed Ali in Alexandria. He was raised almost entirely by his mother after his father remarried and left for work in Saudi Arabia, and his childhood involved many different moves and homes. He and his brothers ended up in the small coastal town of Agami, a funky beach community west of Alexandria known to be the holidaying spot of a liberal, wealthy, film- and arts-inclined crowd from Cairo. There, Wegz attended a public high school that changed his life. Among his schoolmates was Elsayed Agami, an up-and-coming R&B singer. He and Wegz became fast friends, and this was his foray into music. Wegz began to experiment with rap, developing a knack for the genre, and making a swift mental decision to take music seriously ("I didn't want to just be rapping to my friends," he told a talk show host). One friend led to another, and Wegz was soon skipping school to jam with Alexandrian rappers who were already uploading their tracks online. His own first single, "TNT," which he made during his freshman year in college in 2018, riffed on being self-taught as a rapper, and in it, he pronounced himself and his crew as "the next generation of rappers." It was uploaded by the artist Dinho, who had taken Wegz under his arm, promoting him, taking him in with his crew, and featuring Wegz's music on his page. "TNT" was popular, and Wegz started to gain his own followers. He left Dinho on amicable terms to do his own thing.

Wegz quickly made a name for himself. His lyrics were smart and catchy; he was following in fellow Alexandrian Pablo's footsteps and writing his own words. One song, "Hawary," mapped out what it meant to have grown up in poor alleyways. Another, "Kan Nefsy," was a poignant rap about a breakup. Although he sometimes rapped about drugs, Wegz never came off as trying "to be bad." He was endearing, and soulful. And while his music was squarely situated in the world of rap and trap, Wegz also seemed to be borrowing from other genres, including the ever-popular *rai*. His audience was growing, and the potential for its reach seemed vast. When asked in an interview around this time who he learned from, his response was "no-one." Dinho had been dissed, and a battle between the two began. "I still see you below me," Wegz rapped at Dinho in one of those songs.

Wegz was the scene's new, young breakout artist, so when in 2020 he released the single "Hustla," about a fellow musician "having things easy," a guy who thinks he is the "real deal," fans wondered: Who was he dissing?

> You're confused, why, you slog and slog and never reach
> Your corrupted stories make my stomach turn
> Who are you, really? Wegz, I'm the real hustla
> I worked so hard until they said you've changed your core
> Money breeds madness, palms they fill
> To the face tell me, where you settle
> Your hearts are shrouded in rust with envy

50   The single was released online and circulated among social media networks and music pages, and in a matter of hours, everyone was talking about it. Everyone who knew and followed the scene understood the song was a takedown of Abyusif. Anticipation was high. Would Abyusif ignore it or diss back? He rapped back, of course, with the song "Okay," two weeks later:

> Okay, Okay
> Yo driver, on the beat, I cut you in two halves
> To be wrapped in cellophane and made into a bouquet
> I forgive, I don't forget, I don't depend, No names
> Tesla, like my eyes, what color should I get
> On fire with me, so in winter a cup
> Yo driver, this is the summit, and you ain't here . . .
>
> . . . I thought you were the real deal, but you failed like this, how
> They called you to the party to fill the space
> After that you come and spin to Mexico
> And I tell you, at the time, Yo driver, C'est la vie
> You've lost the plot, you don't know who you are
> I beat you, and for you the average is a vitamin
> I won't see you, I don't deal with rogues
> I won't beat you, I don't fight with girls

Wegz's diss was about Abyusif's privilege, but Abyusif's retort not only gave it back ("I don't fight with girls") but even roped in other rappers, among them another popular up-and-comer called Marwan Moussa, who was often taken down himself for having a German mother and having lived abroad (in

Rome and Los Angeles). This double-whammy diss took the beef to the next level. Rather than answering back with songs, Wegz took to Instagram, with live-feeds and stories, dissing, mimicking, and putting Abyusif down. He was responded to in kind. This went on for weeks, and young Egyptians were captivated to the tune of millions of views. It was a chaotic three-way war, as Marwan Moussa took a dig at Wegz, too, poking fun at a real incident when the rapper was kicked out of a gated compound on the outskirts of Cairo. "Hey dude, get yourself together so I don't report you to the security of Beverly Hills again," Moussa posted on Instagram. Abyusif elbowed back at Moussa for not following up with his own diss track, to which Moussa responded underhandedly, implying he was too busy for this child's play since he was in Dubai recording.

Moussa finally released the song "Kolo Fil Saleem," ("Everything in the Safe"), dissing Wegz for being a "creatively challenged two-faced kid," and Abyusif for being a "jerk." Then he posted another song, "Mesh Okay" ("Not Okay"), a direct answer to Abyusif's first track. Abyusif's response was a huge hit called "Megatron," while Moussa answered with "Megatroll." The prolific back-and-forth gave fans the same kind of thrill that perhaps only football has before. Loyalties were won, sides were changed, and new fans were made. Opposing worldviews and sets of experiences had finally met, in an equal playing field of beats and lyrics. The genre was transforming from the voice of the underdog into something broader, cutting across social classes and circumstances.

Mohamed Ramadan

It is impossible to write about *mahraganat* without addressing the issue of Mohamed Ramadan. The singer came onto the scene late, in the shadow and footsteps of a popular duo, and without the skill possessed by many of his younger peers. Neither is he dedicated to the form, or to music at large: the dark-skinned, curly-haired, skinny-legged, wide-chested Ramadan was an actor before anything else; a fame he sought from a young age.

Ramadan, who is in his mid-thirties and grew up in one of the poorer neighborhoods on the periphery of Cairo near the pyramids, dropped out of school to seek acting workshops, where he won attention as a student. Although he was rejected by the theater academy, he showed up at movie set locations trying to get auditions, and began to get cast in Arabic films as a teenager. He secured roles across a whole spectrum of movies, from the cheaply made to the more cinematically proficient, such as *Scheherazade, Tell Me a Story*, by the award-winning

Egyptian filmmaker of international fame Yousry Nasrallah. "I remember being at an audition with him," one former actor said of Ramadan. "I was cast in a small role, he was given a big role. And when I asked why, the director, who was a family friend, turned to me and patted my back and said, 'This boy has real talent, raw.' We both auditioned, and as we came to leave, I realized that he was going to take several buses to get home, and he wasn't that far from where I lived. He had nothing, no money, he was so modest and simple and a nice guy. I gave him a ride, we chatted about life, he said we should keep in touch. I didn't ever think he would make it in the way that he has. He was really a nice kid at the time."

But what Ramadan came to want was "private jet" kind of money, as he is quoted in an early interview saying. The key to that would be mass appeal—lowbrow, high-grossing movies over the more refined, beautifully cinematographed films of Nasrallah. The Sobky brothers, who had a popular butcher shop in the working-class neighborhood of Mohandiseen before venturing into the entertainment industry, were producing the types of films that grossed millions. The offerings were crass, hyperbolic, with the kinds of story lines that involved drugs, guns, and gangs. They were just the kind of movies Egyptians wanted, to escape the realities of economic struggles and political repression. The Sobky brothers signed Ramadan on, making him one of the highest-paid actors in the country.

In 2018, *mahraganat* was exploding into the mainstream, and at friends' encouragement, Ramadan turned to rap. His songs were run of the mill, technically and content-wise. He

54   dealt with girls, money, and even the coronavirus, but not in any
      reflective way. His COVID song, for example, goes like this:

> Come on
> I'm the prince, I'm a gentle man
> I wear a mask and also wear gloves
> I say hello far away without hugs
> Corona Virus, I'll stay safe like that
>
> I'm the prince, I'm a gentle man
> I wear a mask and also wear gloves
> I say hello far away without hugs
> Corona Virus, I'll stay safe like that
>
> Corona rona-rona-rona Virus
> Corona rona-rona-rona Virus
> Corona rona-rona-rona Virus
> Corona rona-rona-rona Virus
>
> We're worried for you about what's happening and what
>   we're seeing
> An epidemic came to us and we don't know what to do
> Clean your hands before you shake the hand of the person
>   next to you
> hey you, who salutes everyone, don't let the nest kill you
>
> Keep people around you safe, dear
> Say that you're keeping you house and family
> Corona is everywhere Corona is my enemy
> I sterilize myself before it enters my body

Come on, come on, come on
An illness affected everyone "what's this, what's this?"
We walk with alcohol "what's this, what's this?"
As we found its name God, God, God
We God's help, we'll find the solution God, God, God

We're worried for you about what's happening and what
      we're seeing
An epidemic came to us and we don't know what to do
Clean your hands before you shake the hand of the person
      next to you
hey you, who salutes everyone, don't let the nest kill you

God, God, God
Corona Virus
Corona Virus
Corona Virus
Corona Virus

The song could be mistaken for a public service announcement, and like a PSA, the repetition was jingoistic. Ramadan's
words were flat, his tunes and beats simple, in many cases even
copied and simply given a twist. His music videos were cut-
and-pasted in terms of scenography and sequencing; all the
ideas were borrowed or recycled. But songs like this immediately became popular, largely on the back of Ramadan's acting
fame. He didn't offer anything innovative musically, but what
he did do, with immense impact, was set the standard for what
every rap artist from Egypt started to want. "I'm obsessed with
power and prestige," Ramadan said in a TV interview. His social

56   media feeds, which show little of his music, are simply a display
of wealth. He has a fleet of the most expensive cars in the world,
a collection of luxury watches, and is always on a private jet.
These types of photos make up the bulk of his Instagram feed.

The flaunting of such wealth in the way Ramadan began to
do was new to Egypt. It ran contrary to common cultural norms,
as well as to the deeply ingrained and groomed belief in the evil
eye, which cautions against any type of boasting or display of
riches. Such flaunting was always considered distasteful, and to
be ignored. But articles about him in the Arabic press are now
seldom ever about his music, but rather about what he owns, as
well as how much his designer outfits cost. He is regularly flown
to Saudi Arabia, Kuwait, and Qatar by wealthy Gulf states and
their princes, and details about the trips make for tabloid
fodder. For a night of performing a song or two, he can fly home
with a Bentley, a gold- and jewel-studded watch, or a check with
many zeros on it. Rappers reference him as the king of the life-
style they want, even as they don't consider him part of the
mahraganat clan. "He has forgotten his origins," an early sup-
porter and now critic said of him. "Here is a kid who came from
nothing. His music is really fast and easy pop, if you will. He
doesn't rap about the kind of things that really speak to people.
But he has set the benchmark for the kind of money you can
make."

Early in June of 2022, Ramadan released his summer single
"Tanteet"—the word means to jump around. The music video,
which is partially set in a casino owned by the Egyptian billionaire Naguib Sawiris—Ramadan calls him "my best friend"—
features the superstar dressed in a ruby-red tux and black

cowboy hat, striding in, pistol in hand. As he takes in the room,
and begins to jump around, he sings:

> No, who said I wasn't coming back
> I was just going to make you take your own time
> I was getting something and coming back
> What I'm hinting at is this
> Yes, I was tired, let's make it clear
> And with the ink of my pen, I will erase it
> I'm coming, make way, make way
> I just said I was getting something and I now I've come
> To complete the planning
> Time away, it doesn't make a difference to my reputation
> Now it's time to dribble
> Jump, jump, jump
> Jump, jump, jump
> Jump, jump, jump
> Jump, jump, jump

The song, which reached 10 million hits in just five days, was cast off by hard-core rap and *mahraganat* fans as "fluff" and "pop disguised as rap." But despite this, to the backdrop of Egyptians expressing their grievances amid backbreaking inflation, an Arabic hashtag calling on Ramadan to run for president briefly circulated on Twitter. Here was a self-made man with little traditional rap-star talent who had molded himself into one of the most galvanizing figures in Egypt.

Ramadan's popular appeal is to the chagrin of mainstream Egyptian establishments, including the Musicians Syndicate,

58   the Ministry of Culture, as well as Dar Al-Iftaa, the country's highest religious authority that establishes moral codes of conduct according to Islamic jurisprudence. Their disdain for Ramadan is partly about the crass manner by which he conducts himself, disregarding Egyptian cultural and moral norms (like showing off shirtless and flaunting women), as much as it is the power he has over his tens of millions of fans. In an episode of the popular national talk show *Secret Ink,* the TV host Ibrahim Eissa said of Ramadan: "Nobody understands social media like him. The country needs to take advantage of this skill. If the country wants to appeal to the youth, if they need a message to reach the masses, the gateway is Mohamed Ramadan."

This popular appeal is threatening precisely because Ramadan seems only to care about the purchasing power his money affords him, rather than how he can use his status and wealth to contribute to society. In social conversations and in the local media, he is continually compared to the Egyptian football superstar Mohamed (Mo) Salah, who is seen as a role model, where Ramadan is not. "Mo" has given back to the country, building hospitals, schools, and even donating money to animal shelters. "Mo Salah has bettered himself with his money, used it to educate himself and do good in the world, whereas all Mohamed Ramadan does is show off," one television presenter said.

Over the past year, Ramadan has repeatedly boasted on social media of his friendship with Sawiris, whose family is considered "old money elite." Last summer, Sawiris hosted Ramadan to perform at Silver Sands, his exclusive gated summer-resort compound on the North Coast of Egypt, which has been bought into mainly by moneyed, Western-educated high-society. Residents of the compound were not happy about the concert, describing Ramadan as "vulgar," "offensive," and "not the example we want our children to have around." On Facebook, one woman whose family owns a villa on the resort, wrote: "If Naguib continues down this path [with Ramadan] I will sell my Silver Sands villa."

Beginnings

Where and when this genre of music began in Egypt is traced largely to the mid-aughts, to low-income neighborhoods where space is limited and outdoor venues like parks or clubs don't exist. Such districts are built around haphazard networks of narrow alleys, dead ends, odd curves that turn into corners. Tiny shops line building entrances selling basic supplies—vegetables, livestock, fresh eggs, pasta, pencils, plastic rulers, and copybooks. Known in Arabic as *manatiq shaabiya* ("areas of the local people"), such neighborhoods make up the majority of the urban city in terms of the population housed. Life here revolves around the shared alleyways between buildings. It's where children play hide-and-seek, football, hopscotch, or most recently, "corona"—a game of tag, where the person tagged becomes the COVID-carrier. The alleys are where events take place—funerals as well as celebrations. Women still string down baskets from windows for neighborhood vendors to fill with goods. Conversations take place across windows. Football matches can be watched almost communally given the close proximity of one building to the next.

Weddings also take place in the tight spaces between homes, most often filling entire neighborhoods, which are decorated with tea lights, strobe lights, shimmery confetti, and tinsel. Everyone does their part, decorating their building or section of the alley. There is no such thing as a guest list—in these close-knit communities everyone is welcome, even expected, as well as anyone who happens to be passing by. Recorded music blasts from speakers—Arabic pop and some Arabic classics. Musicians on the traditional Arabic guitar (the *oud*) might perform for a procession, along with men on traditional drums (*tabla*) and a recorder-like instrument made from cane (*arghoul*).

The emergence of cyber-cafés, "cyber" in Arabic slang, began to change this. In 2002, Egypt's then—communications and information technology minister, Ahmed Nazif, launched a nationwide initiative to make the internet "accessible to all." The end goal was a computer in every home, but the first and second steps to achieving that were government-subsidized internet cafés in working-class areas where children attend public schools. Costs were low—you could spend an hour online for just £E5 (25 cents). Almost everyone could afford, at the very least, a fifteen-minute slot. They began to pop up two, three, four "cybers" to a street, and the change they brought was immediate. Exposure to the West took on new dimensions: shops started to be renamed with foreign words, hairstyles changed among the youth, and fashion slowly started to take what was thought of as an "Americanized" slant—blue jeans and Gap knockoffs appeared here and there.

62   But it was music—easy to make and copy—that was the first big flux-effect of "cyber": synthesized *tabla* with oriental tracks merged with electronic loops mixed on basic programs online—Mixcraft was a favorite. Young men started experimenting with their recordings by putting them on YouTube and checking the number of likes. People downloaded the songs onto thumb drives and played them off neighborhood speakers and out of taxis. Eventually, one could hear this new music more frequently at weddings, usually later into the night, once the procession and traditional songs and vows and customs had been completed.

       This early generation of artists had begun to find audiences in their communities, among people who related to the lyrics that were being sung, and they were doing it live, rapping atop pre-recorded tracks. The beats were partially familiar—often electrified versions of oriental melodies that had been played across generations, but now with lyrics that were of the present. Some of the earliest rappers, like Amr Haha, Alaa 50, and Sadat, started getting gigs. "We were being paid to perform at weddings in neighboring districts," said Sadat, one of the first stars of this yet-unnamed genre.

       Although versions of the history vary according to whom you speak to, Mahmoud Refaat, the founder of the independent label 100 Copies, is most frequently credited with discovering and giving the genre a chance. A pioneer of ushering experimental music artists into the mainstream, Refaat had begun to catch wind of the trend, and had spent hours online browsing uploaded music. He had seen a recording of a wedding, tracked down the artists, and invited them—Sadat, DJ Figo, and Amr Haha—to perform at a downtown theater during a three-day event. In the programming and brochures, he had come up with the term "electro-shaabi" (shaabi meaning "of the people"). This was 2006. It was the birth of the genre, before it had enough of a following and audience to change names and become *mahraganat.*

Mahraganat, which comes from the word *mahragan,* means "festival." For anyone who participated in the eighteen days of protests in 2011 that led to the ouster of Mubarak, those early days of the revolution, when people camped out in Tahrir Square, certainly had the feeling of a festive event (although it can't be formally considered a festival). Ramy Essam, then twenty-two years old, was one of the singers who brought the concert to the heart of the revolution. During the height of the uprising, Essam performed in front of the millions of Egyptians gathered in and around the square. He got up on a small platform set up for political manifestos, brought out his classical guitar, and started to sing. Slowly, the entire square had his attention. He scribbled down his lyrics at night in the tent he shared with friends while camping out in Tahrir. His song "Irhal" ("Leave"), became an anthem to the revolution:

> We're all one hand and we have one demand
> Leave Leave Leave
> We're all one hand
> And we have one demand
> Leave Leave Leave
> Down, down with Hosni Mubarak!
> Down, down with Hosni Mubarak!
> Down, down with Hosni Mubarak!

64   Down, down with Hosni Mubarak!
      The people demand
      The fall of the regime
      The people demand
      The fall of the regime
      The people demand
      The fall of the regime
      The people demand
      The fall of the regime
      He will leave
      We won't leave
      He will leave
      We won't leave
      He will leave
      We won't leave
      He will leave
      We won't leave
      We're all one hand and we have one demand
          Leave Leave Leave

Essam became one of the musical voices of the uprising, and when Mubarak finally stepped down on February 11, 2011, the song "Sawt Al Horreya" ("The Sound of Freedom") was played on every TV, radio, and satellite channel. It was a return to the power of music as it had existed historically in Egypt—the Arab world's greatest and most beloved star, Umm Kulthum, sang songs in celebration of Egypt's independence from Great Britain, in praise of King Farouk, and later, after the revolution that overthrew the monarchy, she sang several dozen political songs themed around then-president Nasser and his policies.

Although she wasn't the only singer dealing with politics, she perhaps set the trend, and was by far the most revered.

Along with colleagues at a small magazine we edit called *Bidoun,* we were led to Sadat and Amr Haha one day in Tahrir Square, performing in a corner, riffing on the streets about the revolution and what the people wanted—essentially, why they, too, were there ("in search of a better life"). We interviewed them at the time, and invited them to perform at an event we were organizing in London at the Serpentine Pavilion. Sadat was just eighteen. He had no money. Getting him a passport and a travel visa was an ordeal, since he had no mailing address and none of the formal documents that were required. To get to Tahrir Square, he took several buses from the housing project where he lived, which had been built to house the refugees of the 1992 Cairo earthquake. He could hardly believe that someone might actually pay to fly him to London, and certainly we had no sense at the time that this genre would become so popular. But these young men, who had next to nothing, wove words and phrases together with beats so brilliantly that they stuck in your head.

Like most other rappers, Sadat and his crew also sang about drugs and sex, but their main theme was the lack of cash, and when they rapped about women, they were bemoaning marriage-related problems, such as not having the means to start a family. These were the types of things one was hearing young people speak about in Tahrir Square, too. The majority of them weren't really there for the downfall of a dictator—they were there because of the lack of basic needs.

As the revolution began to falter, Sadat also rapped about the return to the status quo. His lyrics tackled police brutality, political assassinations, corruption, and the chaos of the Muslim

66   Brotherhood's rule. He called it "the abyss," "all in the name of
religion." He didn't stop there, taking on the military next. Sadat
became as much beloved, by millions of fans, as he was despised,
by citizen patrols, as well as the regime itself. He had followed in
the footsteps of Ramy Essam, as much revered by the people as
he was despised by the state.

The events of 2011 had been the impetus for millions of
Egyptians to purchase smartphones, making internet access
widespread in a much more immediate way via 3G. Social
media became a means of sharing information, and within
months of Mubarak stepping down, the number of Egyptians
with Facebook, Twitter, and YouTube accounts skyrocketed.
Young writers, artists, and musicians were putting out their
work on social media platforms—YouTube, SoundCloud, even
just files on Facebook Status updates. "There was an incredible
sense of freedom," said Sadat. "Everything was changing. It
was liberating." At the time, you could hear *electro-shaabi*
tracks streaming out of both poor and mixed-income neighborhoods. Young people were hearing themselves in the lyrics,
and in that way, being heard. The music was spreading, but still
kept out of the formal mainstream for its "vulgarity," and the
ill-ease it instilled. In an interview with the filmmaker Salma
El Tarzi, Ortega said of the genre: "We have four social segments in Egypt: Poorer than poor, poor, middle class, and
upper class. We are happy to be part of the poorer than poor,
but we do and sing as we want."

Crackdown

Egyptian *mahraganat* with all its variants of rap and trap has been seeping into public consciousness for almost a decade now, but if there is one song that is to be credited with putting *mahraganat* into the mainstream and onto the minds and tongues of even the more privileged and educated "upper classes" who have long shunned the genre, it is without question "Bent El Giran" ("The Neighbor's Daughter") by Hassan Shakosh:

> The neighbor's daughter has raptured my eyes
> When I'm in a place, that's the trance around me
> I don't want anyone to notice the state I'm in
> I saw the moon and she has me up late nights
> I'm dying for you, God knows
> Leave your window open, why close it
> Like a pastime you stay with me
> Your eyes are my mirror and what a pretty one

68   Stay! If you leave I'll call for you
        You for me and me for you, the both of us
        If you leave me I'll hate my life and my years
        I'll be lost drinking alcohol and smoking hashish
        And if you come you'll find me well
        You won't be for anyone else, there's no one else but me

The song was released on January 27, 2020, and reached 120 million views on YouTube and several million listens on other sound platforms in just a few weeks. Egyptians educated in English or abroad, people who had never spoken of *mahraganat,* were suddenly discussing the song. Even young children, too young for these trends, were singing it under their breath, many of them too little to understand what it was even about. The song had that catchiness—compelling in its rhyme, in how its words were so easy to remember and then roll off the tongue. Just two weeks later, on Valentine's Day, 75,000 tickets were sold out online within hours of the announcement that the song would headline a show at Cairo Stadium.

Shakosh was a football player before he turned to music. He played on the B-League Egyptian team Ismaily SC, and those who followed him have said that with enough support he might have gone further, perhaps as far as to play on the national team alongside Egyptian star Mo Salah. But money was an issue. He didn't have the resources or sponsorships necessary to continue in the sport, with required expenses for training, nutrition, and even equipment like cleats, which wore out quickly. To support himself, Shakosh took jobs repairing shoes, then in carpentry, before eventually starting to dabble in music: "My longtime friend was already making music, and so I joined him, we started to make things together." His friend was Omar Kamal, a soulful Egyptian singer with a growing following and fan base.

Shakosh and Kamal came from simple backgrounds in working-class districts of Cairo, and brought together a senti- mentality and softness that was complementary. Kamal had made mostly love songs until then. As a duo, their content remained similar but their tempo and beats mixed up a bit, moving more into the genre of rap but still easy to listen to. Their drums and electronic beats didn't pound into the ears like other artists in the genre. Technically, they were skilled, and had a way with words. Shakosh took to writing and riffing about life in his own neighborhood. The duo's songs were popular, but nothing prepared them for the impact of "Bent El Giran."

By the time Shakosh woke up the morning after his Cairo Stadium concert, his life, and the entire music scene in Egypt, were turned upside down. Although "Bent El Giran" had been out for weeks already, the performance of it in a stadium owned by the state seemed to cause a breaking point. Government officials condemned the musicians for encouraging immoral behavior and tainting cultural and social norms. Egyptian rap- pers had been singing about drugs, alcohol, girls, and even political taboos for years by then, but the fact that the concert was held at the same venue as the country's most important football matches, and even attended by top-tier public offi- cials, was seen as something of an endorsement by the govern- ment. It was also streamed to tens of millions, on TV and online. Although they weren't the only singers performing that night—others included pop stars such as Tamer Hosny and Nancy Ajram—they were, with "Bent El Giran," the reason the crowd went wild. Young men and women screamed for an encore, singing along at the top of their lungs and chanting for the song to be played again.

In the following days, one public official after another came out in condemnation, not just of Shakosh and Kamal, but of the music genre as a whole. Parliamentarian Salah Hasaballah went so far as to say that *mahraganat* was even more dangerous than the potential threat of COVID coming to Egypt. Other members of parliament followed suit. Arabic newspapers and news magazines ran headlines about the blasphemy of the genre and this song in particular, describing it all as "music of the slums." Facebook and Twitter—the most popular social media platforms for Egyptians—were abuzz with debates around the government outcry. The offending line that had prompted this outrage was also one of the shortest in the song: "If you leave me I'll hate my life, I'll be lost drinking alcohol and smoking hashish."

Then head of the Musicians Syndicate, Hani Shaker, was quick to toe the government line. Although he had previously intimated that *mahraganat* was a genre of its own and might receive licensing under a new section of the syndicate, he now issued a statement banning *mahraganat* artists from performing in any festivals, clubs, cafés, or concert venues. As the official body governing music in the country, he effectively outlawed *mahraganat*. The statement he issued read:

> To all touristic venues including Nile boats, Nile-side venues, Cafés, effective immediately a ban on dealings with music artists in the genre of *mahraganat*. And who is found in violation, will be subject to legal punitive measures, as issued in accordance to this legal statement and ban.

In an interview that night with the talk show host Amr Adib, Shaker said, "*Mahraganat* musicians will no longer be working in Egypt. They will not be able to obtain licenses to perform. This type of music is based on promiscuous and immoral lyrics, which is completely prohibited, and as such, the door is closed on it. We want real art." Shaker cited a list of names in recent violation of the requirement that every performer obtain a concert license. Among them was Mohamed Ramadan, who also was banned. "This type of music, this genre, does not represent Egypt," he said. "This is a final decision. There will be no licenses for this style anymore. Only a few artists have passed the syndicate's tests, and they will be banned too." The Syndicate then released a separate statement about Omar Kamal, noting that, although he had been licensed for four years by then, his license was now revoked.

But none of this could have been a surprise to Shaker—this song, its lyrics, and the popularity and fans it commanded. It had been blasting from every taxi, radio, and café for weeks in the lead-up to the concert. What had changed? Why the sudden attention to its lyrics? "Shakosh and Kamal had given me their word that they would change the line 'I'll be lost drinking alcohol and hashish,' and they still sang it," he said. Although Shakosh claimed that it was the DJ's mistake—that it was a playback version and the wrong one was played—the decision on the part of Shaker and the Syndicate was final.

The decision was reinforced across different media. In a national TV interview in the days following, well-known composer Helmy Bakr, a decades-long gatekeeper for Egyptian music and the head of several committees that administered singing tests for the Syndicate, radio, and TV, said: "The music kitchen is now full of cockroaches and insects, and no kind of insecticide would help." Government entities, including the Ministry of Education and Dar El-Ifta, didn't put it as crudely, but generally agreed.

It seemed as if this musical revolution of *mahraganat*, with its free-wheeling lyrics and the political and social freedom it brought, would end as fast and hard as the political revolution that birthed it had. Radio stations, TV channels, internet platforms were all issued statements by the Musicians Syndicate not to broadcast *mahraganat*. Newspaper columnists began to lament the decline of the morality and values of this upcoming generation of Egyptians, and they applauded the Syndicate for its strong stance. It still wasn't clear just how this ban would be implemented, with music uploaded to international platforms such as YouTube and Soundcloud. Many popular music channels were broadcasting on satellite—from Turkey, for instance. How would the government control what people were listening to in private, even if it could control venues it licensed?

In the weeks following, it became apparent that it would be impossible to entirely ban and silence these music artists. Every taxi, street-side café, and *tok-tok* seemed to be streaming "Bent El Giran," as loudly as they possibly could. The song's ratings went up; online viewers and listeners hit 100 million in a couple of days. Shakosh was rumored to have made close to $750,000 from the song's YouTube viewings alone. Everyone was talking about it, debating the value of free speech, even in this new space of cultural taboos and despite the fact that the genre had its fair share of detractors. It toed a fine line for Egyptians invested in culture—if an entire genre of music could be banned, eventually that could happen to cinema and

literature. Questions and concerns likes these seemed to be
everywhere, even on Egyptian private radio. *Should young people
be left to talk openly about alcohol? Should drugs be discussed?
Should the content of songs be controlled? Isn't it better to discuss
these topics in public rather than hide them and pretend they don't
exist? True, this is against our culture, our value system, everything
we have known, but can we keep denying it, given that we all know
it exists?*

This was not the first ban on performers of its kind, nor would it
be the last. Young singers including Ramy Essam of Tahrir
Square, and the *mahraganat* stars Sadat and Shobra ElGeneral,
have long been living in exile, because of the state's threats
against them for their political lyrics. Essam was tortured by
Egyptian state security before he was able to flee Egypt in 2014,
and lives in Finland and Sweden, and Sadat and Shobra ElGeneral
live in France. The ever-popular Mohamed Ramadan has also
been penalized and banned for various offenses, including
cozying up to an Israeli singer in Dubai. During a performance
in the Saudi Arabian capital of Riyadh, he bounded onto the
stage wearing only a Saudi headdress and pants as he sang "I Am
King." The Saudi social media sphere was incensed—he went
shirtless in a conservative culture where even men (at the time)
were not expected to bare skin, and he was cited for referring to
himself as "King" in the Kingdom itself. The Egyptian government relies on the Saudis for financial support, and it was suggested that Ramadan had violated a prior agreement signed
with the Syndicate to abide by performer regulations, including
not removing his clothes when onstage. Although Ramadan was
not a member of the Syndicate, his Saudi performance was cast

74   as a violation of his agreement. And in 2019, *mahraganat* musicians were banned from performing at the upscale beach resorts of Cairo's North Coast, on the back of a request spearheaded by the country's Westernized elite, who shunned the genre as vulgar, and feared what its presence in their backyard might mean to a particular way of life, and to their summer escapades.

For several weeks after the Valentine's Day concert, public attacks on performers were rife, not just finger-pointing references to drugs or alcohol, but any jab the media could find. Marwan Pablo was skewered on television for a "blasphemous" riff on the words of the Sufi Al-Naqshabandi while performing in a duo with a Palestinian rapper. He was also criticized for wearing Adidas Yeezy shoes that cost several thousand Egyptian pounds. TV hosts used these criticisms to suggest that he, and others like him, weren't a good example for Egyptian youth. Double Zuksh and his friends were bashed for posing with semiautomatic guns, and Mohamed Ramadan was heavily criticized for being a bad example with his materialism and the flaunting of many women at once. He was called foul-mouthed and "from the garbage."

Some artists lobbied the Syndicate to reverse its decision. By mid-March, in a partial reversal, it was announced that *mahraganat* artists would be required to attend an audition and interview with the department's listening committee, which would decide whether the quality of the performances warranted a license or not. It also reserved the right to revoke any licenses in the event a performer broke the rules dictated by the new department. The license included a morality clause. Where, when, and how they could perform, and what they could sing, were to be under scrutiny and control. The only artist who had seemed to slip through these cracks was Wegz, who Shaker described as "educated," "someone my son and wife listen to," "a graduate of the American University in Cairo" (he is not), and "not of the *mahraganat* genre."

The most popular and high-grossing artists hadn't waited around for the reversal. They were already performing again, not in Egypt, but overseas. Hassan Shakosh, Omar Kamal, and Mohamed Ramadan were being flown as far as to the United States, and on private jets to Qatar, Dubai, and Saudi Arabia. They were paid handsomely, put up in luxurious suites, and gifted with luxury goods. It was the younger up-and-comers like 3enba who were willing to do acrobatics to get another chance. What exactly would the singing tests entail? Until they were licensed, they were banned—so they wondered if anyone would get the license at all, and in a country that's known for its massive bureaucracy, everyone wondered aloud how long a licensing might take.

Finally, in November 2021, over a year after the initial ban, the Musicians Syndicate released a list of artists who were not permitted to perform. Number one on the list was a rapper named Hamo Bika, who had been criticized for wearing chunky gold chains and (according to critics) "looking like a drug dealer." Even though he doesn't rap about drugs, the Syndicate seemed particularly chagrined about his presence in the field. Although Bika had already passed the vocal test process undertaken by the Syndicate, he was banned for not meeting the standard of a "presentable image of Egypt." According to Shaker, Bika was "banned from performing due to behavioral issues." The singer was furious, and in an interview he said: "How do these people see me? Do they think I'm some pest or piece of garbage? . . . I'm sorry, with all due respect to Mr. Hani Shaker, I am a human being."

Number five on the list was 3enba—young, and not yet making the kind of money that would allow him to leave Egypt and tour. He appealed to the Syndicate for another chance. They approved: no lurid lyrics, no political talk, no riffing about drugs, weapons, or anything "culturally offensive." He had to submit to a complete rebranding of who he was. Although he doesn't formally admit it, the Syndicate is likely the reason he changed his stage name from 3enba to 3enaabb. (Members of the Syndicate also implied as much but would not state so directly.)

But not everyone was happy. When 3enba was hosted on the grounds of an army-operated venue in an upscale residential neighborhood several weeks after he was relicensed, anticipation was high as to who might complain and what might unfold. The neighborhood was outraged that his rowdy fans had crowded the streets around the theater. The police said they received eighty-seven complaints that night, the fire department twenty-two, and eight formal cases were registered at the police station against the performance, citing noise levels, crass culture, and the fact that *mahraganat* should not be allowed in a residential neighborhood. The concert was eventually shut down, and as lights dimmed on the stage, 3enba said, "because of the residents of this neighborhood."

Residents debated raising a society-based law case against both 3enba and the venue. Such a case would be a citizen complaint, which would be put before the public prosecutor. Egypt has seen many such cases in recent years. The novelist Ahmed

Naji was jailed for ten months following a citizen-based complaint of lurid sexual scenes in his book. Given the already contested atmosphere, such complaints to the public prosecutor could put 3enba and those like him behind bars.

One week later, the same venue was advertising for another 3enba concert the following month. On a neighborhood WhatsApp group, members expressed outrage, and immediately started planning a campaign to ban these types of performances once again. "Can anyone please call Faiza Abou El Naga," one member asked, referring to the former Mubarak-era minister and current advisor to President Sisi, who also happens to be a resident of the neighborhood. Another resident began asking others to file legal cases against the club. Another set up a meeting with the district MP. The club was shut, temporarily, even though 3enba still held his valid performer's license. But he had to perform elsewhere, and it hasn't been as straightforward as he and others had hoped. At the time, venues reported being wary of bringing artists like him, and really any *mahraganat* artists, onboard. "You never know when they're going to be banned again and it's going to immediately reflect on us," said a manager of Blue Nile, a popular restaurant that also hosts singers several nights a week. "It's also a difficult situation, because while they have their fans, it also means we lose another kind of sophisticated clientele who won't go to a venue that also hosts and supports *mahraganat*. That clientele is generally higher-paying. If they come for an event, they eat and drink at a much higher price point. These are all things we have to consider."

Future

On June 2, 2022, a group of "concerned citizens" met with the governor of Cairo in his office in an annex of Abdeen Palace, the seat of government until the revolution of 1952. Among those in attendance were several former ministers, a member of parliament for several southern Cairo districts, and various community leaders, including a prominent banker. The impetus for the meeting was a reported surge in hooliganism that was impacting residents in a central Cairo neighborhood. All those in attendance said their families were directly affected. Over the course of the meeting, several files were presented documenting problems associated with the masses of young *mahraganat* fans roaming the neighborhood after concerts, taking over entire streets to play their music, dance, and drink late into the night. "We don't feel safe anymore," they told the governor. "We don't let our young girls walk in the streets alone in the evenings anymore," one former minister said.

The governor, Khaled Abdel Al, who was formerly the chief of Cairo Security, asked the necessary questions, and looked closely at the evidence. Among the files presented was a video of a group of twenty young men forming a line across a residential street, *mahraganat* blasting from their stereo. A woman tried to cross their path, but they moved to block the pavement where she was approaching. She retreated, shouted, and turned to take another route. Another CCTV video showed crowds of young men gathered outside buildings and on side streets, with music playing loudly. They rolled joints and lit them, and beer cans and vodka-mix bottles are strewn around them. Occasionally they harassed women walking by—one young man grabbed a passing woman's arm. In one video, a security guard from a nearby cultural center asks such a group to leave. A policeman arrives later and asks them to leave. Eventually, the policeman goes, and the gathering stays. By morning, the area is littered with empty bottles and garbage. The policeman, when asked later about the incident, says he has no power against these young people anymore. None of the incidents seem to surprise the governor. He simply nods his head—this is a problem he has become familiar with. He promises to send more police onto the streets.

In the aftermath of COVID, after the long lull of empty streets, these scenes have suddenly become commonplace in many neighborhoods across Cairo. Young men, loud music, and alcohol and sometimes drugs—this is new to Egypt, at least in such a public way. Generations like mine, and the ones that came before it, were constrained—careful about the parameters of a culturally conservative society centered on a patriarchal system that everyone feared: concern for what elders, the government, the police, and the community might think. But this way of thinking, this upbringing, these social values (or pressures) with their upheld ideals, now seem obsolete. Here is a young generation who make up the majority of Egypt's population, who are loud, expressive, and fearless of all the norms and expectations that have traditionally kept society in check. Even the very basics of an orderly city and community—going the right way down the street in a car or on a bike, throwing rubbish in garbage bins, observing rules of where alcohol can or cannot be consumed—such details are no longer given thought to, or are of consequence. In my own neighborhood, young men throw stones at passing girls, toss empty fast-food bags and containers on sidewalks, and blast music under residential buildings deep into the night. When one tries to reason with them, they often laugh, getting a kick out of the interaction. They turn the music up. This is a generation that grew up in the shadow of the revolution and its failures, in an atmosphere plagued by defeat, and in many ways, it has found its attitude, its strength, its fearlessness, and also its growing anger, in the echoes of lyrics that reflect that letdown.

When I set out to write about the *mahraganat* scene several years ago, I believed that the music was spawning a movement that would generate political change. It seemed like a vast and important shift; this young generation of artists who were speaking about realities and opinions that preceding generations had been too fearful to explore publicly. Here, finally, was a sizable segment of the population being vocal about long-shunned subjects: relationships, sex, drugs—issues that exist but were never deemed appropriate for general conversation. What was more striking was their willingness to talk about the political realities suffered by tens of millions of Egyptians—the

economic hardships, inequalities, and the extreme control of
public opinion and debate. It was a massive break from the past,
from anything that even my generation had ever known. It
seemed like the core ingredient for change would be what was
conceived in Tahrir Square: the ability to discuss problems
openly, publicly, with resonance. Only then could a public consensus be gained, and solutions collectively reached. Music
seemed like a solid starting point.

That hope has been complicated in part due to the rule of
President Sisi, who has constructed a parallel system to the government that is commanded by the army and steeped in censorship and control. Although the music scene has been somewhat
uncontrollable, with its reliance on international platforms like
YouTube, SoundCloud, and Spotify, every other means of public
debate and expression has been quashed. The hope for a pluralistic political system was given up on long ago—when the president ran for reelection, every potential opposition candidate
was threatened, arrested, or otherwise intimidated by the state.
All opposition, which is a prerequisite for a healthy political
environment, has been all but shut down. Public consensus no
longer matters to the government. (In a recent interview, Sisi
said that "the country is being rebuilt and the stories of individ-
uals can't factor into that equation.")

There is perhaps no more evident illustration of this than
in the actual restructuring of the city—the bulldozing of
neighborhoods, the rezoning of residential districts, and the
taking-over of public space in residential neighborhoods for
commercial use and to the benefit of the army. In the neighborhood of Dokki, home to the Ministry of Agriculture, several public gardens were taken over and turned into complexes

82 and strip malls of cafés. When residents in the area complained, they were told "it's for the public good." A letter was
drafted to the president's office, suggesting that the residents
of the neighborhood are in fact that "public," and these cafés
were not for their good, but it received no response. The same
has happened in residential neighborhoods including Zamalek,
Heliopolis, and even the newer suburbs and satellite cities like
6th October City and Sheikh Zayed.

Across the country, starting in its capital, Cairo, residents
have been alienated from their neighborhoods due to vast construction projects that have cut through or completely demolished or disfigured them. In tandem, Egypt has been subjected
to a series of economic reforms and development projects that
have placed it, and the population, under immense financial
pressure. A new capital, built to replace the old administrative
districts of Cairo, has cost the government $59 billion to date.
It is still far from complete, and running well over budget.
Located twenty-eight miles outside the city, it has also required
the retrofitting of new highways and bridges to ensure that the
old road network leads there, a cost estimated at $4 billion so
far. That doesn't even include the $4.5 billion price of the lon-
gest monorail in the world. Much of the historic center of
Cairo is being bulldozed to the ground and built anew. Art deco
buildings are being replaced with skyscrapers, seventeenth-
century neighborhoods are being razed and replaced with new
replicas of them, ancient cemeteries are being demolished to
make way for roads. The Nile banks are being turned into concrete walkways. Every empty plot of land from the coast to the
city center is being turned into a development of one kind or
another—tens of thousands of new homes are being built in

gated communities, many under an arm of the government or the army. They are branded with foreign names and advertised with massive English-language billboards. And on the Mediterranean coast, the number of apartments, villas, chalets, even sky-scrapers, is inexplicable. Economists say it's a "bubble."

With the country already struggling economically given its limited production (staples such as rice and wheat are now all imported) and its vast population, Sisi's "development" boom— at the expense of healthcare and education—has placed Egypt in debt. One economic advisor to the state, also a former deputy prime minister, said he had "never been as worried about Egypt economically as now." Egypt keeps borrowing from the IMF and Arab states, and as subsidies on basic commodities are lifted (gasoline, bread, and electricity had all been heavily subsidized), and the Egyptian pound is floated and keeps dropping against the dollar as a precondition of the IMF loans, inflation is sky-rocketing. Life has become prohibitively expensive for the majority of Egyptians. Even the more privileged complain of rising prices—supermarket costs are often compared with those in Europe. Greece, Portugal, and even London are often cited as cheaper places to buy food. "The thing with Egyptians is that they will constantly compromise on their quality of life, and that's how the country keeps going. But until when?" the economic advisor said.

This expansive redevelopment of the country has placed the government under the spotlight, in particular since the army is making planning decisions and expenditure choices without consulting either citizens or at times even relevant government institutions or ministries. Egyptians have come to track who buys what and what the president is wearing and how

84   much his watch, his son's house, or his relatives' palatial homes and luxury cars might have cost. This applies to all those in his service. As the government and its circle of contractors, developers, and army generals make huge profit margins on all the construction in the country, the wealth gap widens. Dozens of gated compounds sell villas with starting prices of $1 million. On the long stretch of the northern coastline, the cheapest beach property starts at half a million dollars and some go upwards of $10 million. And on the roads of the city, Range Rovers, which cost £E5 million, have become commonplace. "We're talking of a new class of billionaires, not millionaires," a former newspaper publisher and columnist told me. And that wealth is out on the streets for everyone to see.

In the summer of 2019, when a former owner of a contracting company who worked on construction projects for the army started to post videos revealing government spending on infrastructure from his self-imposed exile in Spain, his YouTube uploads went viral. The government sent out an international arrest warrant for him, but he kept posting. When he started calling on Egyptians to protest, the government initiated a widespread crackdown on political dissidents in Egypt. A few, including the former newspaper journalist Khaled Dawood, have only very recently been released. Many of those arrested remain in jail.

More and more, the situation feels like a political time bomb. Extreme wealth is being rubbed in the face of a vast youth population who have no means, and no real chances of making a living. Jobs are hard to come by, and wages are generally low. "The country can't keep up and can't provide," the advisor said. "You have a segment of the population with nothing to hold onto."

The only thing they *do* seem to have, and hold onto as a symbol of hope, are their music stars, whose shoes they want to fill. But even there, the music, which was once an outlet, seems to have become the source to stir up further anger and frustration—these sentiments and energies are very tangibly simmering. Before and after concerts, on the once highly patrolled streets of Cairo, hundreds of young men turn to drugs, alcohol, and perhaps most simply and tellingly, a kind of hooliganism that has encroached on neighborhoods and the safety citizens feel on their streets. After one concert, young men drank beers on a dark street and threw the empty glass bottles against a building wall, bursting into hysterics as the bottles smashed and splintered everywhere. Motorcycle engines were revved up on sidewalks, with little regard for pedestrians who had to dodge out of their way. Groups of young men roam the city's streets, sporting hairdos of their favorite artists. They wear designer knockoffs, and with caps of Coke cans they scratch fancy cars that they see parked—their reasoning is that if a person can afford an £E2 million car, then surely they can afford to fix a scratch. They sing lyrics—the parts about drugs and money—as loudly as they can.

At the local police station, the director admits: "The problem is that they have no fear, and we don't have much power. In the past, under the emergency law, we could arrest anyone. We can't anymore. We get phone calls of complaints daily about these young men, but unless you catch them actually sniffing a drug, you can't even arrest them for having just taken it." They also have some troubling role models. In late July in Alexandria, a car driving against traffic down a main street was stopped by a traffic police officer. The driver laughed, and

86 responded: "Don't you know who I am?" It was *mahraganat* star Hamo Bika.

Over the course of a few years, before and then after COVID, as I found myself becoming increasingly uncomfortable around these groups, what I came to realize is that for the majority of these youth, the music unleashes the energy that is pent up—of grim futures, of unmet material wants, and of a sense of futility in imagining a tomorrow any different from their current situation. "Life is about today," one fan in a group of young men told me, his friends nodding in agreement beside him. "I'm twenty-two, and there is no future, so let me do what I want today." That translates into roaming the streets, listening to music, throwing things. "I throw bottles because it feels good," he says. "It's like a release."

For all the government's promises of "development" and "job creation," they have entirely overlooked the country's largest demographic—this population of media-savvy, Western-influenced, under-twenty-five-year-olds, who largely have no contract jobs and no formal benefits (unemployment in the fifteen-to-twenty-nine age bracket stands at 62 percent). The problem is further complicated by the fact that the army controls a vast and growing segment of the economy. Over the past three years, since Sisi secured his second term in office and passed an amendment to the constitution to allow him to stay in power even longer, businesspeople have repeatedly complained that they are facing unfair competition from army-owned companies and factories. Although no one will speak on the record, it is widely known that the army has built new factories in major industries next to privately owned ones, forcing business owners to downsize, and in many cases, shut shop. "The army isn't subjected to the same market rates for raw materials, nor does it pay taxes, so when they set up a mirror factory to mine down the street, of course I can't compete," one business owner in the textile industry said. "They eventually stole our top technicians, since they could hire them away from us at much more competitive rates." That businessman has since shut down his factory, and is selling off its material assets. Although international pressure has been put on the president to withdraw the army from the economy in part through the privatization of army businesses (most recently that pressure has come from the IMF), so far little concrete progress has been made. Credible rumors abound about a leadership struggle at the top tier of army ranks.

The state, under President Sisi, is perhaps best described as version 2.0 of Gamal Abdel Nasser's Egypt—a regime that believes in taking from the people for the benefit of the country. But while Nasser's Egypt tried to please and appease the poor, and for the most part succeeded, in the case of Sisi, every segment of society has been subjected to his iron fist for the sake of the future. Egyptians have lost residential properties, factories, businesses, agricultural land, desert land, even floating houseboats—all in the name of "development" and the "public good." As the army gets richer, the people quickly get poorer. Everyone is feeling it. On the back of public spending and borrowing, inflation is in double digits, and the Egyptian pound is plummeting in value.

The most impacted segment of the population is in many ways the youth, who are bombarded with the displays of the wealth that exists, aware of the vast spending on projects that

88   will not serve them, and alienated from the kinds of jobs the
army is creating that they either lack the technical skills for, or
do not aspire to (such as being laborers on construction sites).
Walking through the streets of Cairo, Alexandria, or governorates like Ismailia, Port Said, and most recently Minya, the energy
of discontent and frustration is palpable. These youth are the
same everywhere—impacted by the way the nation overlooks
its citizens. It is no surprise, in the face of this, that the street
has become the hangout for these young people, and that they
unleash their anger in revving and racing motorbikes, in bottles
thrown at walls, and increasingly, in drugs, alcohol, and a general hooliganism. This phenomenon is familiar globally, but it is
new to Egypt, with its once-conservative norms of conduct.
Even the banks of the Nile, once free to roam for everyone, have
been "developed," at a cost of many millions of dollars, into concrete walkways that are limited to ticketed entry.

Videos of Mohamed Ramadan on his private jet get circulated virally on music-fan platforms and on TikTok, and some
mahraganat singers get hundreds of thousands of "likes" on
social media posts where they pose with guns and money (even
if fake). It is no surprise, in short, that young people feel frus-
trated, that there is no sure way to work their way out of poverty,
toward the lifestyles that they are taunted with, by their government first and foremost. As talk show hosts on Egyptian television channels have been repeating in recent months, stories of
crime, murder, and rape are on the increase. "This is not the
Egypt we have known," prominent TV host Lamees Hadidi said
on a recent program. "Guy murders girl because she refuses to go
out with him. Man slaughters wife and buries her in the garden.
Guy threatens to kill girlfriend on the university campus. What

has become of us? How has it become so easy to just kill? What
is this new Egypt?"

This "new Egypt" ("the new Republic" is Sisi's refrain) represents the breaking down of a society and the collapse of cultural norms. It is a time bomb, not in the political sense of waiting for a revolution, but in the much more frightening threat of how a culture becomes overrun with violence, crime, and fraud. Strangers have taken to knocking on doors, claiming to be government employees, asking to inspect electricity or gas meters, building pipes or fire extinguishers, and demanding money in return. Egypt has always been known as a place safe enough to walk in any neighborhood in the deep of night, but that seems to be fast changing, at the hands of youth, and the politically precipitated economic crisis. More and more, I hear people say they don't feel safe walking alone in the streets at night. One parliamentarian says he won't let his teenage daughter in the streets alone at any time of day. Even in once-privileged neighborhoods, like Zamalek, where I grew up, residents are taking caution. "A friend a few buildings down asks me to escort her if she needs to go down in the evening," a former minister said. "She doesn't feel safe. It has, in reality, become unsafe." What will become of this? Can it be contained or diverted? Where will the country go?

Early in 2022, as the Egyptian economy tanked to its highest debt level in history, and speculation was rife about the country defaulting on its foreign sovereign loans, the president announced the launching of a "national dialogue." What this would mean wasn't clear, except that it was indicative of the government taking note of the growing discontent. A series of forums were set up in the weeks that followed, supposedly

90   bringing Egyptians from across all walks of life together in an
ongoing conversation about the state of the nation. Even though
this dialogue has purportedly begun, none of it is being released
publicly. So those not privy to the discussions all wonder what
the outcome will be. *Will political dissidents be allowed to speak
freely again? Will press censorship end? Will military trials for
civilians end? Will political prisoners on fabricated charges be
released? Will the armed forces back out of the economy? Will citizens be compensated when their apartments are taken as buildings
are bulldozed to make space for an extra lane of highway? Will the
army be held accountable for taxes? Will constituents' needs and
opinions on their own neighborhoods be considered in public planning and projects? And will a serious initiative for taking young
people off the streets and into generative activities be considered
and launched? What about education and healthcare and investing
in them over the ongoing infrastructure and development projects
across the country? What about the exorbitant taxes, pocketed by
the army, on private property, on personal imports, and even on
licenses to start small businesses?* The questions awaiting answers
have no end.

At the start of the Egyptian academic year that began in October
2022, the government issued a blanket ban of *mahraganat* music,
as well as on weapons and "tight" clothing on university cam-
puses nationwide. The rules covered anything "inappropriate":
too tight, ripped, distressed, see-through, along with shorts,
flip-flops, and leggings. *Galabiyas* were also banned. "Weapons"
included fireworks and flares, alongside knives and guns. A
note against eating, smoking, or drinking in lecture halls was
also included in the statement, and although it was not directly

stated, it was assumed to mean alcohol. The country's most widely watched television hosts all took the issue up on their nightly segments, debating the necessity for this kind of control, but also asking aloud what had happened to Egyptian society: "The values of our society are broken," was the most frequent refrain. When I posed the same question myself on the streets, in the supermarket, in taxis, as I went about my days doing errands, government paperwork, relicensing my car, paying my taxes, the same set of answers were repeated. More often than not, I was told: "Mohamed Ramadan wrecked everything," and in the same breath, "The country is wrecked anyway one way or another—they wrecked our homes and lives with their projects and these prices."

As Egypt negotiated a new bailout package from the IMF last fall, which involved a proper float of the currency, which has historically been pegged to the dollar, prices increased again. In the course of two days, the Egyptian pound lost 35 percent of its value. Headlines spoke of shortages of rice, chicken, eggs: not because they weren't actually available, but because traders were hoarding supplies, in order to release them later at higher prices. People began to murmur about "bread riots," and what the revolution of hunger might look like.

In early November, in the days leading up to the COP27 climate change conference hosted in Sharm El Sheikh, twelve high-ranking members of the intelligence services and army resigned from their posts, and another twenty were fired, with some placed under house arrest, according to credible sources. Ahead of a national football match, the government ordered all cafés and public spaces shut down from early afternoon on that day,

92   fearing what might happen if fans were left to spill out onto the streets. This all came ahead of calls for protests on 11/11, against Sisi, his rule, and above all, his spending. Police and plainclothes informants circulated the streets of Cairo, checking mobile phones and arresting people at random. A journalist and two lawyers were taken at night, one directly from the airport on his return from a conference in China, and the others from their homes. The government ordered the country to "shut down" on November 10, starting at 3:00 p.m. — cafés, businesses, shops. In a phone-in intervention to a TV presenter, the president ranted about lack of gratitude on the part of Egyptians. He also stated that he had no money to upgrade the education system, and suggested that the billions of dollars being spent on the infrastructure of the country would bring in funding that could be put back into schools. He warned against criticism, implicitly stating that his intelligence services are listening in on everything.

Against the backdrop of this tense political atmosphere, the recently appointed new head of the Musicians Syndicate, Mostafa Kamel, once again banned *mahraganat*. His case was aided by bans on Mohamed Ramadan performing in places like Qatar and Syria (on moral grounds). But other artists felt the ban was unfair, especially as new rules that were subsequently announced required rap artists to have twelve "authorized" musicians accompanying them. Debates abound about whether the decision is right or not, and generally, around the fate of this both loved and hated genre.

When the ban was announced, I was traveling outside of Egypt, and with the political climate so fraught, and many rumors circulating that the president might be internally ousted, I was unsure what to expect when I returned home after two weeks away. But when I arrived in Cairo and left the airport, heading on the main road that leads from the airport to the center of town and running right by the Presidential Palace, the first billboard that greeted me was a Rotana advertisement for Mohamed Ramadan. On social media I take note of someone's comment that "everyone just follows the money." Ramadan knows this, and sings in an Instagram post about money being his pass to everything. One of his latest songs is called "Dawsha," or "Noise," and the music video is simply that. Ramadan is more and more a subject of debate across social circles for his public conduct: except for the very young, consensus seems to be that he doesn't serve as the kind of role model Egyptians expect of someone of such stature and fame. The Syndicate informally echoes the view—they expect musicians to be moral leaders for society at large. It's a noble cause in some sense—wanting younger generations to have good role models—as much as it is a problematic one: a strategy of control, with its various methods of censorship and outlaw.

When I wrote this, just ahead of the November 11, 2022, protests, the country's most carefully scripted narrative for COP27 was falling apart. Egypt's most prominent human rights defenders—the government's harshest critics—received the biggest audience in Sharm El Sheikh, with the international media spotlight focused on the one issue the country had hoped to suppress: political prisoners, and in particular Alaa Abdel Fattah, who timed a dry fast in prison to coincide with the commencement of the conference. With such pressure, it was anticipated by many that he would be released, as an international gesture of publicity and goodwill. (He was not.) Public officials

94 lied about his conditions on the record to the press, and although Alaa's case is historically divisive in Egypt, criticism of the government's handling of it, in particular during COP, has been ubiquitous.

On the streets, I hear people complain about the cost of living and, in the same breath, about the president. In my neighborhood, plainclothes informants seem to be everywhere again, reminding me of the weeks and months that led to January 25, 2011. While many people I know are being more cautious about what they say and where they go, placing mobile phones in other rooms during dinner conversations, the youth seem not to be concerned—they come out onto the streets in throngs each evening, playing loud music and loitering as they always do. Although these young Egyptians have a stellar role model to follow and aspire to in the likes of the rising international star Wegz, and even in his trailing peers Marwan Pablo and Abyusif, it is too much of a gamble of luck to follow in such footsteps. The mire of the current state of affairs, with its rising costs, is also not an aide. It seems likely, once again, that a confluence of forces—of Egypt's massive youth population and the country's economic and political woes—is edging toward an implosion of one kind or another, at the very least of the social fabric and cohesion of the country as we have long known it to be.

I would like to start by thanking the team at Columbia Global Reports: Jimmy P. So, Nicholas Lemann, Camille McDuffie, and Allison Finkel. Thank you, also, to Emily Lavelle.

In a political environment as fraught and oppressive as Egypt is, it is always a risk for people to speak openly about their opinions and experiences. Politics and art collapse into one for the Egyptian citizen; they become inseparable. Although this project is ostensibly about a music scene, in reality it is much more so about a political landscape. The music becomes a way to write about politics. I am grateful for the many dozens of people who spoke to me on these terms: politicians, public figures, publishers, newspaper editors, journalists, critics; economists, bankers, businesspeople; night-life operators and their teams of staff; sound technicians, set managers, artist managers, music producers, venue managers, corporate sponsors; musicians, videographers, bloggers; curators, gallerists; community organizers, civil servants, members of the police force; contractors, architects, urbanists, and engineers. I depended on a rotating cast of young liaisons of sorts—students, recent graduates, and others dabbling in the music scene—for access, information, and at times to go where I could not. Even if there were not too many people to name, many would remain unnamed for their protection, and in many cases, on their own request. The same goes for the tens of dozens of youth I spoke to informally, on the streets, on the sidelines of concerts, at cafés. This book is really about them—their lives, their futures—and without them it would not have been possible.

There has been so much already documented about the *mahraganat* scene, and I read and watched as much as I could. The notes in the back of the book are a partial reference.

I am grateful for DCAF, Townhouse Gallery, and Rawabet for the creative space they have provided and nurtured over the years.

Sadat, Amr Haha and DJ Figo were my entrée into *mahraganat*, and for them I am grateful.

Thank you, Salima Barakat, Nada Mobarak, Mai Al-Ibrashy, Nadra Zaki, Negar Azimi, Clair Wills, Amira Howeidy, Sarah Rifky, Aleya Hamza, Sara El Adl, Mahmoud Khaled, Walid Ghoneim, Yasser El Shamy, Tawfika Tewfik, Farida Makkar, Fadia Badrawi, Samir Hammam, Lynnette Widder, Joseph Slaughter, Mila Turajlic, Elizabeth Rubin, Laurie Fitch, Mai El Dib, Maaza Mengiste, Tash Aw, John Freeman, Amy Atwood, Omar Kholeif, and Andre Aciman.

Thank you, Bidoun and *Bidounis*.

Thank you, Zoe Pagnamenta.

Thank you, Nathan Brown.

I was lucky enough to spend time at Columbia University's Institute for Ideas and Imagination in Paris as I wrote through an earlier version of this manuscript—time that was a gift. I'm indebted to the entire team there, especially Marie d'Origny, Carol Gluck, and James Allen. Thank you also to Brunhilde Biebuyck and Mark Mazower.

Thank you, Mamdouh El Rashidi and Malak Ahmed (aspiring future president of Egypt).

Thank you, especially, Nevine Hussein and Seif El Rashidi.

Modern Egyptian history has produced a somewhat divided body of academic and literary texts geared for a mainstream readership, reflecting opposing views of historical events—in particular on revolution. This reading list tries to be comprehensive, not in the sense of offering an exhaustive selection of books, but rather, in offering a varied, at times idiosyncratic, reading of a contested set of histories.

That Smell by Sonallah Ibrahim. This is actually a novel, published in 1968 in the aftermath of Egypt's defeat by Israel in the Six-Day War. It tells the story of a recently released prisoner and his malaise as he struggles (and fails) to readjust to everyday life on the outside. It captures the sense of stasis and oppression that has pervaded Egyptian life since Nasser's time, when the novel was written. The novel is a good scene-setter for understanding what daily life feels like in the country under an authoritarian regime. It also illuminates what the current youth generation in Egypt are breaking away from.

Bread and Freedom: Egypt's Revolutionary Situation by Mona El-Ghobashy. One of the best accounts written on the Egyptian Revolution—at once scholarly and deeply researched and recorded, as well as a literary read.

The Arab Winter: A Tragedy by Noah Feldman. For a comprehensive reading of the events leading up to and through 2013, and more broadly the Egyptian Revolution and its aftermath, this book is an excellent source, and a great companion read to El-Ghobashy. Feldman offers a point-by-point narrative of the progression of events, offering both his own reading and position, as well as alternate and opposing ones.

Radius: A Story of Feminist Revolution by Yasmin El-Rifai. A powerful and affecting portrait by one of the organizers of the anti-harassment movement in Tahrir Square. This account also offers the opportunity to reflect forward onto the current moment, and the kind of harassment women continue to face.

Whatever Happened to the Egyptians? by Galal Amin. Written by an economist and academic, and blending hard facts, personal anecdotes, and a necessary dose of humor, this book is essential reading to understand in simple terms the economically rooted social, cultural, and religious shifts that began to unfold after the Revolution of 1952.

98   *Soldiers, Spies, and Statesmen: Egypt's Road to Revolt* by Hazem Kandil. Reads almost like a spy novel. For anyone interested in the details of the deep state (the military, the intelligence, and the government) with all the maneuverings of power, intrigue, and backstabbing that led, eventually, to 2011, this book is a must.

Understanding Cairo: The Logic of a City Out of Control and *Egypt's Desert Dreams: Development or Disaster?* by David Sims. Critical reading as companion books, the first to understand the informal settlements that have sprawled around the outskirts of Cairo, and which are the original home to many young rappers, and the second to get a feel of the extent to which the government is spending on desert developments. The book was published before the current government under Sisi began to spend billions on its new administrative capital and other such megaprojects, but it lays the groundwork for the problem at large.

Cairo the City Victorious by Max Rodenbeck. A compelling biography of the city, as much about its history as its character, spirit, and the culture that defines it. It helps understand the immensity of Cairo's scope—politically, economically, culturally, and simply as a sprawling urban environment.

The Voice of Egypt by Virginia Danielson. A rigorous and compelling biography of the most influential singer and personality in the Arab world, perhaps to this day, Umm Kulthum.

Translating Egypt's Revolution: The Language of Tahrir edited by Samia Mehrez. A collective project that translated and interpreted texts, signage, chants, speeches, manifestos, and more that grew out of Tahrir Square and the revolution of 2011.

NOTES

INTRODUCTION

10   **Gamal Abdel Nasser (1956–1970) was well known for his method of having people disappeared:** For background on that refrain, see: https://timep.org /commentary/analysis/behind-the -sun-how-egypt-denies-forced -disappearances.

10   **[Nasser's] persecution of Egypt's Jews:** For a brief timeline: David D. Kirkpatrick, "A Timeline of Jews in Egypt," *New York Times,* June 23, 2015, https://www .nytimes.com/2015/06/24/world /middleeast/a-timeline-of-jews -in-egypt.html.

10   **deep state, with its troops of secret police and informants:** For more on the deep state and Mubarak's human rights record, see Amnesty, starting with: https:// www.amnesty.org/en/latest/news /2020/02/hosni-mubarak-legacy -of-mass-torture/.

11   **Egyptian government's broadcasting arm:** Known as Maspero, this was the symbolic center of media power: https:// en.wikipedia.org/wiki/Maspero _television_building.

12   **The Egyptian Revolution of 2011:** For my account of the uprising, see *The Battle for Egypt, Dispatches from the Revolution.*

12   **up to 60,000 political dissidents were being held in jail:** Vivian Yee, "'A Slow Death': Egypt's Political Prisoners Recount Horrific Conditions," *New York Times,* August 8, 2022, https://www .nytimes.com/2022/08/08/world /middleeast/egypts-prisons -conditions.html.

12   **the long-standing "emergency rule" measures:** Although the formal nationwide state of emergency was ended on October 25, 2022, the government incorporated emergency-like measures into other laws, effectively perpetuating the long-standing state of emergency, https://www.hrw.org/news/2021/11 /05/egypt-emergency-provisions -made-permanent.

12   **stated on television that he will never allow what occurred in 2011 to happen again:** "Text of Al-Sisi's Speech During the Activities of the Egypt Economic Conference 10/23/2022," http:// manassa.news/stories/7728.

12   **Alaa Abdel Fattah, a blogger, computer programmer, and activist:** For background, Yasmine El Rashidi, "He Was Detained. That Didn't Stop Them From Kidnapping Him," *New York Times,* October 3, 2019, https://www .nytimes.com/2019/10/03 /opinion/egypt-Alaa-Abd-El -Fattah-protests.html.

13 Muslims formed human chains around Coptic churches across the country: Yasmine El Rashidi, "Egypt's Muslims Attend Coptic Christmas Mass, Serving as 'Human Shields,'" *Ahram Online*, January 7, 2011, https://english.ahram.org.eg/News/3365.aspx.

14 On New Year's Day 2011: Yasmine El Rashidi, "In Egypt, Activism Escalates, Spurred by Tunisian Riots and Local Violence," *Ahram Online*, January 1, 2011, https://english.ahram.org.eg/NewsContentP/1/2982/Egypt/In-Egypt,-activism-escalates,-spurred-by-Tunisian-.aspx.

14 30,000 protesters had gathered in Tahrir (liberation) Square: For my account of January 25, see Yasmine El Rashidi, "'Hosni Mubarak, the Plane Is Waiting,'" *New York Review,* January 26, 2011, https://www.nybooks.com/online/2011/01/26/hosni-mubarak-plane-waiting/.

15 they chanted, mantras such as the most popular refrain, "bread, freedom, social justice": From PBS, see "Egyptian Protesters Chanting in Tahrir Square," *PBS NewsHour*, YouTube video, February 4, 2011, https://www.youtube.com/watch?v=i23N1x3Hhco.

16 and its message in the chants and songs that accompanied it: For more on this, see Karima Khalil's book *Signposts from Tahrir.*

16 judge sentenced 683 alleged Muslim Brotherhood members to death in a single trial: David Stout, "Egyptian Court Recommends Death for 683 Muslim Brotherhood Supporters," *TIME,* April 28, 2014, https://time.com/78955/egypt-court-death-sentences-muslim-brotherhood/.

17 "family principles and values upheld by Egyptian society": Basil El-Dabh, "Egypt's TikTok Crackdown and 'Family Values,'" Tahrir Institute for Middle East Policy, August 13, 2020, https://timep.org/commentary/analysis/egypts-tiktok-crackdown-and-family-values/.

17 practice of "citizen patrolling": Yasmine El Rashidi, "How Egypt Crowdsources Censorship," *New York Times,* December 8, 2018, https://www.nytimes.com/2018/12/08/opinion/sunday/egypt-censorship-crowdsourcing.html.

17 content posted by local social media influencers: Ciao Deng, "Egypt Arrests Social media Influencers in Deepening Crackdown," *Wall Street Journal,* February 11, 2023, https://www.wsj.com/articles/egypt-arrests-social-media-influencers-in-deepening-crackdown-b26835bc.

17　**social media users with more than 5,000 followers are considered "media outlets":** "Media Law in Egypt: The New Developments," Youssry Saleh & Partners, March 25, 2018, https://youssrysaleh.com/Investment-in-Egypt/media-law-in-egypt-the-new-developments/.

18　**The duo Oka and Ortega:** For their YouTube channel: https://www.youtube.com/channel/UCrB69D12WG5mBhxskz0RNyg.

19　**population had grown by 750,000 in the past six months:** Shereif Barakat, "A 750,000 Population Surge in 6 Months: What Does It Mean for Egypt?" *Egyptian Streets*, August 29, 2022, https://egyptianstreets.com/2022/08/29/a-750000-population-surge-in-6-months-what-does-it-mean-for-egypt/.

CHAPTER ONE

21　**The ancient port city of Alexandria:** For background on the history of Alexandria, read E. M. Forster's book *Alexandria: A History and Guide*.

21　**pushed out the Jews, the Italians, and the Greeks:** For the Jewish exodus and experience, read Andre Aciman's *Out of Egypt*.

22　**Bibliothecha Alexandrina:** Bibliothecha Alexandrina homepage, https://www.bibalex.org/en/default.

23　**to hold a portion of its thirteenth edition in the city:** Retrospective, Documenta 13, June 9–September 16, 2012, https://www.documenta.de/en/retrospective/documenta_13, and "Class Trip: Kaelen Wilson-Goldie on Documenta 13: 'The Cairo Seminar,'" Artforum, July 11, 2012, https://www.artforum.com/diary/kaelen-wilson-goldie-on-documenta-13-the-cairo-seminar-31367.

23　**but the people voted in political Islam:** Yasmine El Rashidi, "Egypt: The Rule of the Brotherhood," *New York Review,* February 7, 2013, https://www.nybooks.com/articles/2013/02/07/egypt-rule-brotherhood/.

24　**Marwan Pablo, first known as Dama:** For the Dama playlist: https://genius.com/albums/Marwan-pablo/Collection-dama.

25　**enrolled him in a language school:** For more on the education system in Egypt, see: https://wenr.wes.org/2019/02/education-in-egypt-2.

28　**"That person technically died," he explained to a music critic:** YouTube video, March 27, 2018, https://www.youtube.com/watch?v=VxawzItM4ac.

28　**The song that Marwan Pablo (aka Pablo) came out with in his rebirth, "El Gholaf X Ozoris":** Marwan Pablo, "El 8olaf x Ozoris,"

102   Soundcloud, n.d., https://
soundcloud.com/user-360913810
/marwan-pablo-el-8olaf-x-ozoris.

30   his solo breakout, "Sindbad":
Marwan Pablo, "Sindbad
(Wardenclyph Remix),"
Soundcloud, n.d., https://
soundcloud.com/wardenclyph
/sindbad-remix.

**32   The video for the song was
shot in Alexandria:** Marwan Pablo
x Molotof, "Free (Official Music
Video)," Vimeo, https://player
.vimeo.com/video/374695194.

**32   "Geb Felos," or "Get
Money," like the 1995 song by
the Notorious B.I.G.:** Pablo x
Molotof, "Geb Felos," Soundcloud,
n.d., https://soundcloud.com
/molotofmusic/pablo-x-molotof
-geb-felos.

**33   But as his listener ranks
climbed:** Marwan Pablo, "CTRL,"
song, Spotify, https://open.spotify
.com/track/2lj1RNDztkIsyzhAX2so
Ea?si=4a2f76e11b784111.

**34   Critics started to refer to him
as the "Godfather of Trap":** For
one reference see Vice video:
"Marwan Pablo: Egypt's Godfather
of Trap," Vice Asia, YouTube video,
October 3, 2019, https://www
.youtube.com/watch?v=wYKEREf
Q3So.

**34   in an advertisement for the
mobile phone carrier Vodafone:**
"The Three Pablos," Wunderman
Thompson, n.d., https://www
.wundermanthompson.com/work
/the-three-pablos.

CHAPTER TWO

**36   Such a case would fall under
one of Egypt's several ambiguously
worded laws:** For the various laws
and civil liberties cases, see the
Egyptian Initiative for Personal
Rights, https://eipr.org/.

**36   on-air via a phone-in with
Amr Adib:** https://www.youtube
.com/watch?v=7no5XUoUzkI.

**37   Musicians Syndicate's
licensing test and procedures:** For
background on such control, see
Lara El Gibaly, "From Constitution
to Law: The Legalities of Making
Art in Egypt," Mada, April 6, 2017,
https://www.madamasr.com/en
/2017/04/06/feature/culture/from
-constitution-to-law-the-legalities
-of-making-art-in-egypt/, and
Sarah Ramadan, "A Closed Door: A
Paper on Membership as an Entry
Point for Independent Artistic
Syndicates in Egypt," Association
for Freedom of Thought and
Expression (AFTE), March 22, 2021,
https://afteegypt.org/en/research
-en/research-papers-en/2021/03
/22/21293-afteegypt.html.

**37   Plainclothes Syndicate
"informers":** For more on this, see
S. Frankford, "Music, Censorship
and the State: The Case of Egypt's
Musicians' Syndicate," University

of Oxford, white paper, https://
www.iaspm.org.uk/iaspm/wp
-content/uploads/2020/09/Sophie
-Frankford.pdf.

38 **banned Sherine from
performing in Egypt:** Mira Maged,
"Sherine Abel-Wahab Banned from
Performing in Egypt," *Egypt
Independent,* March 22, 2019,
https://egyptindependent.com
/sherine-abel-wahab-banned-from
-performing-in-egypt/.

39 **his breakout, "Ibn Al-Balad":**
"Mahragan Ibn El Balad," 3enaba
and Ordony - Topic, YouTube
video, July 6, 2020, https://
www.youtube.com/watch?v
=OWHYa21aNR0.

41 **The median age in Egypt
is 24.6 years old:** "Egypt
Population (Live)," Worldometer
.com, https://www.worldometers
.info/world-population/egypt
-population/.

41 **40 percent of the population
live in informally planned areas:**
Reem Leila, "Safe Relocation:
Egypt's Plan to Eradicate Slums by
2030," *Ahram Online,* February 8,
2019, https://english.ahram.org.eg
/NewsContent/1/64/325213/Egypt
/Politics-/Safe-relocation-Egypts
-plan-to-eradicate-slums-by
-.aspx.

41 **His social media followers:**
https://www.tiktok.com/discover
/3enaab.

42 **In the early months of the**   103
pandemic: Michael Greenberg,
Aida Alami, Tolu Ogunlesi, Merve
Emre Rahmane Idrissa, et al,
"Pandemic Journal, March 23–29,"
New York Review, March 29, 2020,
https://www.nybooks.com/online
/2020/03/29/pandemic-journal
-march-23-30/#rashidi.

43 **during COVID "the current
has changed and it's all about
kites":** "Tayarat," Enaba - Topic,
YouTube video, July 6, 2020,
https://www.youtube.com/watch?v
=4QTHUZWertY.

43 **The single was an instant hit:**
"Popular 3enba Songs," playlist,
Genius.com, https://genius.com
/artists/3enba.

43 **"El Melouk," or "The Kings":**
"El Melouk," Ahmed Saad,
YouTube video, June 23, 2021,
https://www.youtube.com/watch?v
=QbnAqCusrZE.

43 **was featured in an episode of
the Marvel TV show *Moon Knight*:**
Farah Rafik, "Marveling Through
Moon Knight's Genius Soundtrack,"
Egyptian Streets, May 10, 2022,
https://egyptianstreets.com/2022
/05/10/marveling-through-moon
-knights-genius-soundtrack/.

44 **he hung out around a pool at
a villa with his friends:** 3enaabb
on Instagram, July 26, 2022,
https://www.instagram.com/p
/CgfCz8XIcwE/?igshid
=YmMyMTA2M2Y=.

104 CHAPTER THREE

45 **at more widely attended rap-battle festivals:** An example of this form: https://www.redbull.com/int-en/tags/mc-battle.

45 **The diss is a vast platform for growth:** "Battle Rap," Rap Wiki, n.d., https://rap.fandom.com/wiki/Battle_Rap.

46 **took place between 3atwa and Yousef Joker:** "First Rap Battle in Egypt," 3aTwa, YouTube video, February 15, 2017, https://www.youtube.com/watch?v=aoIqT1rD5JA.

46 **The voice of that life—this underclass—was essentially the birth of the genre:** On broader origin: "Going Black: The Commodification of Hip-Hop Culture," *Postscript Magazine,* Issue 16, n.d., https://postscriptmagazine.org/content/2018/12/03/going-black.

48 **"I prefer to think of them as equals":** "Interview with Abyusif," Mostafa Sobhy - Estbaha, YouTube video, January 21, 2022, https://www.youtube.com/watch?v=eq6WK7divvY.

48 **Abyusif's rate of releasing singles:** For an Abyusif playlist, https://open.spotify.com/playlist/37i9dQZF1DZo6evO2zfOwK.

48 **"I didn't want to just be rapping to my friends":** Wegz in conversation with talk show host Soad Younes and singer Ruby.

49 **released the single "Hustla":** "Wegz - Hustla (Audio)," Wegz, YouTube video, November 25, 2020, https://www.youtube.com/watch?v=-h2L426YZGA.

50 **with the song "Okay," two weeks later:** "Abyusif X - Okay (Official Audio)," Abyusif, YouTube video, November 28, 2020, https://www.youtube.com/watch?v=x7vEy8w_Ye8.

51 **Moussa finally released the song "Kolo Fil Saleem":** "Kolo Fil Saleem, Marwan Moussa (Lyric video)," Turquoise, YouTube video, February 18, 2021, https://www.youtube.com/watch?v=BunzGiBBAmI.

51 **Then he posted another song, "Mesh Okay":** "Marwan Mousa - msh okay," Sefeen Maher, YouTube video, March 10, 2021, https://www.youtube.com/watch?v=onQQ_UEklEQ.

51 **Abyusif's response was a huge hit called "Megatron":** "Megatron," Abyusif, YouTube video, February 19, 2021, https://www.youtube.com/watch?v=Gv7Fja_eK8o.

CHAPTER FOUR

52 *Scheherazade, Tell Me a Story: Scheherazade, Tell Me a Story,* Arab Film Festival Australia, YouTube video, May 20, 2010, https://www.youtube.com/watch?v=CDxyS7GT7Yw.

53 **"private jet" kind of money:** Sky New Arabia, https://bit.ly /3DRKv6c.

55 **"I'm obsessed with power and prestige":** Ahmed Maher, "Egypt's Biggest Star Mohamed Ramadan Talks Rags to Riches and Provoking Critics," *The National,* August 1, 2021, https://www .thenationalnews.com/mena/egypt /2021/08/02/exclusive-egypts -mohamed-ramadan-reveals -journey-from-poor-suburbs-to -superstar-success/.

55 **His social media feeds:** Mohamed Ramadan Instagram feed, https://instagram.com /mohamedramadanws?igshid =YmMyMTA2M2Y=.

56 **articles about him in the Arabic press:** One example of thousands, https://gate.ahram.org .eg/News/3758262.aspx.

56 **his summer single "Tanteet":** Mohamed Ramadan, "Tanteet," Soundcloud, n.d., https:// soundcloud.com /mohamedramadanofficial/tanteet; Mohamed Ramadan, "Tanteet," YouTube video, January 26, 2022, https://www.youtube.com/watch?v =5cvUD5qQXB8.

56 **set in a casino owned by the Egyptian billionaire Naguib Sawiris:** Mohamed Ramadan on Instagram, https://www.instagram .com/p/Ch5N3ORIcaf/?utm_source

=ig_embed&utm_campaign =loading.

58 **In an episode of the popular national talk show *Secret Ink*:** Ibrahim Eissa speaking about Ramadan, https://www .almasryalyoum.com/news/details /2721755.

CHAPTER FIVE

61 **nationwide initiative to make the internet "accessible to all":** Ahmed Nazif, "Building the Egyptian Information Society," International Telecommunication Union, n.d., https://www.itu.int /itunews/manager/display.asp ?lang=en&year=2004&issue=03 &ipage=egypt&ext=html.

62 **Amr Haha, Alaa 50, and Sadat:** 100 Copies Music, YouTube video, May 31, 2015, https://www .youtube.com/watch?v=s52_AAc _dKE.

62 **the independent label 100 Copies:** 100 Copies Music Space, Cairo Urban Initiative Platform, n.d., https://www.cuipcairo.org/en /directory/100-copies-music -space.

62 **is most frequently credited:** See, for example, Golia, Maria, Egypt's Mahraganat, Music of the Masses, and Afropop Live interview with Mahmoud Refaat.

63 **he had come up with the term "electro-shaabi":** For background,

106   Passant Rabie, "The Rise and Rise of Electro Shaabi," *Egypt Today,* November 26, 2013, https://www.egypttoday.com/Article/4/601/The-Rise-and-Rise-of-Electro-Shaabi.

63   **Ramy Essam:** Ramy Essam homepage, https://www.ramyessam.com/.

63   **became an anthem to the revolution:** Ramy Essam, "Er7al," Soundcloud, n.d., https://soundcloud.com/ramy-essam/ramy-essam-er7al.

64   **the song "Sawt Al Horreya":** "Sout Al Horeya صوت الحريه Amir Eid - Hany Adel - Hawary on Guitar & Sherif on Keyboards," Amir Eid, YouTube video, February 10, 2011, https://www.youtube.com/watch?v=Fgw_zfLLvh8.

64   **Umm Kulthum, sang songs in celebration of Egypt's independence:** For background, see Léo Pajon, "Umm Kulthum: 'Enta Omri', a Song to Advance Nasser's Brand of Nationalism," *Africa Report,* June 23, 2021, https://www.theafricareport.com/94124/umm-kulthum-enta-omri-a-song-to-advance-nassers-brand-of-nationalism/.

65   **invited them to perform at an event:** "Serpentine Gallery Park Nights 2011: Shaabi-Wedding-Music-Dance-Party," Vimeo, July 22, 2011, https://vimeo.com/92265349.

66   **making internet access widespread in a much more immediate way via 3G:** MC Sadat, El Alamy, and Alaa Fifty Cent, "The People Want Five Pounds Phone Credit," Politics, Popular Culture and the 2011 Egyptian Revolution, accessed January 26, 2023, https://egyptrevolution2011.ac.uk/items/show/228.

66   **He had followed in the footsteps of Ramy Essam:** "This Egyptian musician's passport was revoked for his political songs. He still can't wait to go home again," *The World,* January 10, 2019, https://theworld.org/stories/2019-01-10/egyptian-musicians-passport-was-revoked-his-political-songs-he-still-cant-wait-go.

66   **In an interview with the filmmaker Salma El Tarzi:** For Salma El Tarzi's documentary on Oka and Ortega, https://vimeo.com/236139594.

CHAPTER SIX

67   **"Bent El Giran":** Hassan Shakosh & Omar Kamal, "Bent El Geran," Soundcloud, n.d., https://soundcloud.com/9dtracks/hassan-shakosh-omar-kamal-bent-el-geran-9d-tracks?in=new-a-songs/sets/kotwwvshw560.

68   **120 million views on YouTube:** Fatma Lofti, "Mahraganat: Controversy over

Barring Egyptian Street Popular Music," *Daily News Egypt,* February 23, 2020, https://dailynewsegypt.com/2020/02/23/mahraganat-controversy-over-barring-egyptian-street-popular-music/.

68   at Cairo Stadium: Eslam Omar, "Egypt's Mahraganat Ban Renews Debates over the Popular Genre," *Ahram Online,* February 17, 2020, https://english.ahram.org.eg/News/363656.aspx.

69   Omar Kamal, a soulful Egyptian singer: Omar Kamal, YouTube video, June 16, 2020, https://www.youtube.com/watch?v=cz_jN5flCKE.

70   of the music genre as a whole: Mira Maged, "Egypt's Musicians Syndicate Contacts YouTube, SoundCloud to Take Down Mahraganat Songs," *Egypt Independent,* February 20, 2020, https://egyptindependent.com/egypts-musicians-syndicate-contacts-youtube-soundcloud-to-take-down-mahraganat-songs/.

70   Parliamentarian Salah Hasaballah went so far: Mohamed El Shamaa, "Egypt's Street Music 'More Dangerous Than New Coronavirus,'" *Arab News,* February 21, 2020, https://www.arabnews.com/node/1630976/middle-east.

70   issued a statement banning mahraganat: "Egypt's Musicians Syndicate Bans Popular Mahraganat

Music," *Egyptian Streets,* February 17, 2020, https://egyptianstreets.com/2020/02/17/popular-mahraganat-music-is-now-banned-according-to-egypts-musical-syndicate/.

71   Amr Adib, Shaker: https://www.youtube.com/watch?v=0009BPuYvig.

71   well-known composer Helmy Bakr: "Helmy Bakr opens fire on Mahraganat songs," YouTube video, February 22, 2020, https://www.youtube.com/watch?v=4MX9cI67wrA.

73   Essam was tortured by Egyptian state security: Cristina Burack, "When Making Music Means Torture," DW, September 27, 2019, https://www.dw.com/en/when-making-music-means-torture-and-exile/a-50469721.

73   cozying up to an Israeli singer in Dubai: "Here's Why Mohamed Ramadan's Selfie with an Israeli Singer Is Problematic," *Egyptian Streets,* November 23, 2020, https://egyptianstreets.com/2020/11/23/heres-why-mohamed-ramadans-selfie-with-israeli-singer-is-wrong/.

73   he bounded onto the stage: "Mohamed Ramadan Causes Social Media Stir in 'Half Naked' Riyadh Performance," *New Arab,* November 5, 2021, https://english.alaraby.co.uk/news/mohamed-ramadan

108   -causes-stir-half-naked-riyadh
-concert.

74   **banncd from performing at the upscale beach resorts of Cairo's North Coast:** "The Egyptian Authorities' Grip on Local Culture: The Example of Mahraganat Music," Arab Reform Initiative, August 7, 2020, https:// www.arab-reform.net/publication /the-egyptian-authorities-grip-on -local-culture-the-example-of -mahraganat-music/.

74   **a "blasphemous" riff on the words of the Sufi Al-Naqshabandi:** "Attack on Marwan Pablo because of Al-Naqshabandi," Alghad TV, YouTube video, October 3, 2021, https://www.youtube.com /watch?v=Eya01zbNlYU.

74   **Double Zuksh and his friends were bashed:** https://www .instagram.com/p/CeB4Yo1Ix6o /?igshid=MDJmNzVkMjY=.

74   **announced that *mahraganat* artists would be required to attend:** Yahia Dabbous, "Egyptian Musicians' Syndicate Unmutes Mahraganat Music," *Scene Noise,* June 27, 2021, https://scenenoise .com/News/Egyptian-Musicians -Syndicate-Unmutes-Mahraganat -Music.

74   **The license included a morality clause:** "We Are with Hany Shaker," *Al-Youm Al-Sabe3,* July 27, 2021.

75   **the Musicians Syndicate released a list of artists who were not permitted to perform:** Ati Metwaly, "'Proper Culture': Mahraganat Music Sparks New Controversy," *Ahram Online,* November 23, 2021, https://english .ahram.org.eg/NewsContent/50 /1205/443171/AlAhram-Weekly /Culture/%E2%80%98Proper -culture%E2%80%99 -Mahraganat-music-sparks-new -contr.aspx.

75   **Hamo Bika:** Bika and Kamal were eventually handed one-year prison sentences. "Egypt: Two Singers Convicted on 'Morality' Charges," Human Rights Watch, April 27, 2022, https://www.hrw .org/news/2022/04/27/egypt-two -singers -convicted-morality -charges.

76   **Ahmed Naji was jailed for ten months:** Michael Schaub, "Egyptian Novelist Ahmed Naji, Jailed over the Content of His Book, to Be Temporarily Released," *Los Angeles Times,* December 19, 2016, https://www.latimes.com /books/la-et-jc-egyptian-novelist -20161219-story.html.

CONCLUSION

79   **Young men, loud music, and alcohol and sometimes drugs:** Ali Abdelaty, "Egypt Says Cheap New Drug 'Strox' Threatens Its Youth," Reuters, November 20, 2018, https://www.reuters.com/article

/us-egypt-drugs-idUSKCN1NP
1TH.

80 **revolution and its failures:**
Read *You Have Not Yet Been
Defeated* by Alaa Abdel Fattah.

81 **hope for a pluralistic political
system was given up on long ago:**
"U.N. Rights Chief Denounces
'Climate of Intimidation' in Egypt
Before Vote," Reuters, March 7,
2018, https://www.reuters.com
/article/us-egypt-rights
-idUSKCN1GJ14Q.

81 **Sisi said that "the country is
being rebuilt":** "The First
Comment from Sisi Regarding the
Removal of the Float of the Elderly
Woman in Al-Warraq (video),"
Masrawy, July 3, 2022, https://
www.masrawy.com/news/news
_egypt/details/2022/7/3/2253357
/أول-تعليق-من-السيسي-بشأن-إزالة-عوامة
-السيدة-المسنة-في-الوراق-فيديو-.

81 **actual restructuring of the
city:** Yasmine El Rashidi, "Sisi's
New Cairo: Pharaonic Ambition in
Ferro-Concrete," *New York Review,*
October 16, 2021, https://www
.nybooks.com/online/2021/10/16
/sisis-new-cairo-pharaonic
-ambition-in-ferro-concrete/.

82 **A new capital—built to
replace the old administrative
districts of Cairo:** "Egypt's
Audacious Plan to Build a New
Capital in the Desert," *National
Geographic,* October 18, 2022,
https://www.nationalgeographic

.com/magazine/article/egypts
-audacious-plan-to-build-a-new
-capital-in-the-desert-feature.

83 **They are branded with
foreign names and advertised
with massive English-language
billboards:** See SODIC, as
one popular developer, https://
www.sodic.com/SodicOur
Developments.

83 **the number of apartments,
villas, chalets, even skyscrapers,
is inexplicable. Economists say
it's a "bubble":** "The Egyptian Real
Estate Market," Coldwell Banker
Commercial, infographic, n.d.,
https://coldwellbanker-eg.com
/en-us/cb/home/Upload-Main
-ProtectedAssetMedia-Filename
-8826fc37c00835748fea05468af
9a154.pdf.

83 **(staples such as rice and
wheat are now all imported):**
Abdel-Tawab Barakat, "Policies to
Starve Egyptians: Destruction of
Egyptian Rice, *Egyptian Institute for
Studies,* October 12, 2022.

84 **post videos revealing
government spending on
infrastructure:** Raphael Minder,
"The Man Trying to Stir a Long-
Distance Revolt in Egypt," *New York
Times,* October 23, 2019, https://
www.nytimes.com/2019/10/23
/world/europe/egypt-sisi-ali
-corruption-spain.html.

85 **If a person can afford an £E2
million car, then surely they can**

110 **afford to fix a scratch:** Steven Sameh on Instagram, October 8, 2022, https://www.instagram.com /reel/CjdR2eysWj2/?igshid=Ym MyMTA2M2Y=.

86 **(unemployment in the fifteen-to-twenty-nine age bracket stands at 62 percent):** Zeinab El-Guindy, El-Sayed Gamal El-Din, "Egypt's Unemployment Rises," *Ahram Online,* November 26, 2022, https://english.ahram.org.eg /News/479849.aspx.

87 **to withdraw the army from the economy:** https://www.ft.com /content/03533d92-4a71-43fc -b885-27dcb962d4e8.

87 **inflation is in double digits, and the Egyptian pound is steadily plummeting:** Tamer Madi, "Why Is the Egyptian Pound Plummeting?" *Esquire Middle East,* n.d., https://www.esquireme.com /brief/why-is-the-egyptian-pound -plummeting, and "Fitch Revises Egypt's Outlook to Negative; Affirms at 'B+,'" Fitch Ratings, November 8, 2022, https://www .fitchratings.com/research /sovereigns/fitch-revises-egypt -outlook-to-negative-affirms-at -b-08-11-2022.

88 **into concrete walkways that are limited to ticketed:** Ahmed Kadry, "MP Asks Egypt's PM to Cancel Newly Imposed Entrance Fees on Ahl Masr Walkway," *Ahram Online,* July 20, 2022, https:// english.ahram.org.eg/NewsContent /1/2/471842/Egypt/Society/MP -asks-Egypt%E2%80%99s-PM -to-cancel-newly-imposed -entranc.aspx.

89 **the Egyptian economy tanked to its highest debt level in history:** Mohammed Ayesh, "Arabic Press Review: Egypt's Debt Soars to Record Levels," *Middle East Eye,* April 12, 2022, https://www .middleeasteye.net/news/egypt -debt-soars-record-levels-arabic -press-review.

90 **ongoing conversation about the state of the nation:** Gamal Essam El-Din, "The National Dialogue: Great Expectations," *Ahram Online,* September 15, 2022, https://english.ahram.org.eg/News /476050.aspx.

91 **As Egypt negotiated a new bailout package from the IMF:** Gamal Essam El-Din, "Egypt, IMF in 'Serious' Negotiations Over $5–7 Billion Loan: Head of Parliament's Budget Committee," *Ahram Online,* August 1, 2022, https://english .ahram.org.eg/News/472435.aspx.

92 **the president ranted about lack of gratitude:** "Phone intervention of Abdel Fattah El Sisi President of the Republic during the TV Program Al-Tasi3a," YouTube video, October 25, 2022, https://m .youtube.com/watch?v=6DDzA4 cue-E&feature=youtu.be.

92 **required rap artists to have twelve "authorized" musicians**

accompanying them: Eslam Omar, "Egyptian Musicians Syndicate Sets New Conditions for Authorizing Mahraganat Singers," *Ahram Online,* October 23, 2022, https://english.ahram.org.eg /News/478331.aspx.

93   the country's most carefully scripted narrative for COP27 was falling apart: Ishaan Taroor, "U.N. Climate Summit Turns Awkward for Egypt," *Washington Post,* November 9, 2022, https://www .washingtonpost.com/world/2022 /11/09/cop27-climate-alaa-prison -strike-sissi/.

93   Alaa Abdel Fattah, who timed a dry fast in prison to coincide with the commencement of the conference: Yasmine El Rashidi, "#FreeAlaa," *New York Review,* November 12, 2022, https://www .nybooks.com/online/2022/11/12 /free-alaa-yasmine-el-rashidi/.

Columbia Global Reports is a publishing imprint from Columbia University that commissions authors to produce works of original thinking and on-site reporting from all over the world, on a wide range of topics. Our books are short—novella-length, and readable in a few hours—but ambitious. They offer new ways of looking at and understanding the major issues of our time. Most readers are curious and busy. Our books are for them.

Subscribe to our newsletter, and learn more about Columbia Global Reports at globalreports.columbia.edu.